Heavenly Text
Finding Christ Within

Vol. III

Heavenly Text
Finding Christ Within

Vol. III

By
Nancy Mertzlufft

Edited by
Mary Mueller, J.D.
Sharon Troth, PhD.

Cover designed by Jenny McGee
Watercolor painting by Nancy Mertzlufft

Printed in the United States of America

Heavenly Text,
Finding Christ Within
Vol. III

Nancy Mertzlufft

Copyright © 2010

All rights are reserved. No part of this book may be reproduced, translated, stored in a retrieval system, posted or transmitted, or used in any form or by any means, electronic, mechanical, photocopying, recording, or otherwise, without the written permission of Nancy Mertzlufft

All bible citations and quotes are from *The Jerusalem Bible,* Doubleday. 1966

ISBN 1456423185
First printing December 2010

Acknowledgements

Thanks from the depth of my heart to all those who have touched my life — those on earth and those in heaven. You are all angels to me. All my writings are dedicated to you. You know who you are. I love you.

Contents

Introduction....................i-xii

Wisdom Lessons Begin...................1

Dreams of Awakening..................42

Going Forward..........................65

The Century of Change...............88

More Gifts............................159

The Gift of Patience..................181

Going to the Light...................224

About the Author....................237

Introduction

A little over twenty-five years ago I gave my daughter Pam (21), back to God. She died from leukemia. She received her diagnosis the last of September (1981) and died the first week of January (1982). It was a tumultuous three months with many ups and downs. I have many sad and happy memories. One vivid memory is when Pam woke up one morning with her face paralyzed. Her face looked distorted, her eye drooped. She looked like she had had a stroke. The doctor informed her that the leukemia was in her brain and that she would probably go blind and not be able to speak. She promptly exclaimed, "No way, God won't do that to me. I don't mind dying but I want to see and talk to my family until I do."

During her illness we had the habit of gathering around her bed at night for prayers - praying for a healing. With the new face problem she asked me to lay my hands on her face while we prayed. One night after prayers she announced. "Mom, I think it worked. Your hands felt hot, and I felt a tingling in my face." I agreed I felt something strange. The next morning her face was back to normal and remained so until the day she died. We were all thrilled. Miracle? I think so.

It was not until after her death that I thought about that night a lot. I had many questions. Why was her face healed

Heavenly Text

and not the Leukemia? I knew God had been the Healer but what was my part? I wondered what happened? I tried to piece together the puzzle. I read prolifically: scientific books, religious books, and many personal stories. I searched for knowledge and truth, which opened a door to a new world for me.

I summarize what I now know to be true in the following paragraphs:

***

The earth is but a small part of a vast Universe/ Cosmos. The Hierarchy of the Heavens is made up of many levels and dimensions. The Spirit world encompasses all of them and is real. The world of Spirit is of *"Light."* We can't always see it but it is available to help us at all times. Our job on earth is to learn how to receive this *"Light"* called the Holy Spirit, and to learn how to use it.

All of creation is connected to its source - God, our Father - and has no end. It always was and always will be. All of creation - nature, animal and human - is "energy" created from geometric *"Light"* patterns. We are all connected and are one with God. All is always in flux, growing and evolving.

God has given each of us a spark of this *"Light"* -- a soul. A soul chooses to come to earth in order to evolve spiritually into a "Light Being." Earth is a school to learn lessons. Mankind forgot this, so Jesus Christ came to earth to teach and to show humans that they can become "Beings of Light." He taught that we are united with the Father, that we can become God's sons and daughters by "unveiling His many gifts." Christ learned how to use this *"Light,"* God's power, the Holy Spirit, and said we could

Heavenly Text

too. He told mankind that through this *"Light,"* "You can heal, Speak in tongues, Raise the dead, Move mountains," and much, much more.

Christ also taught that the way to do this is to love God and our neighbor. Christ taught a love of compassion, accepting all as equal. He loved unconditionally. No religions, cultures, or races were judged differently. He taught that life is difficult, that there would be suffering, but that it is possible to overcome suffering and death. He showed there is no reason to fear death. Death is simply a transition into another state of Being.

All humans have seven sacred power light centers (chakras), which are our spiritual wiring and connection to the heavens and to God. They are the colors of the rainbow. When these chakras are balanced, working in perfect harmony, and in complete alignment with the love of God and others, miracles happen. When the heart and crown chakra are united, an eighth chakra is opened and we connect with our soul, our *"Light"* body. This is what Christ did. Christ said, "I myself can do nothing. It is the Father that is within me that does the work. I AM one with God."

Scientific data indicates that the magnetic pulses of the sun and the vibrations of the earth are changing. It is imperative that mankind realize this in order to understand the unfolding of the times we now live in. Massive changes are taking place in our bodies and in the earth. Humans need to realign themselves with the *"Light,"* the Holy Spirit, in order to bring about the balance of peace for humankind and the earth.

We are living in the time Christ spoke of as the "end times." This means the end of our human bodies as we

Heavenly Text

know them and the end of the earth as we know it. (Not the end of the world.) All is evolving rapidly into a profound Newness. We are living in an unprecedented time in history when this gift, this Power, *"Light Energy of God,"* is more prevalent than ever before and is available to ALL. We can become *"Beings of Light."* We can then heal, and be healed. Knowing and believing in this power is the key to eternal life.

***

Scientists say that matter is not only made of many particles but is a string of vibrating energy. Vibration is everywhere. Every atom of every substance is composed of electrons and protons that are in constant electrical motion and cause magnetic vibration - gases, liquids, sound, light - all are just a difference in vibrations. The Sun, our universe, the atmosphere, nature, people, animals, all are "energy" created from geometric "Light" patterns. Each breath we breathe fills us with energy. Energy is everywhere in everything. To me this is what Ephesians 4:6 implies: "There is one Lord, one faith, and one Father who is Father of all, over all, through all, within all." (Sounds the same as energy to me.) Energy is our true source, our connection to God.

I know we all play a part in our health and illness by the use of our energy. It is well known that maintaining healthy energy is a powerful strategy for maintaining health and preventing illness. In time I began to think of energy as the blueprint of the body. I expanded my knowledge of energy by studying energy medicine. (Energy medicine is about the proper flow of energies in the body.) In time I learned that energy medicine can address illness and can also prevent illness. I researched all kinds of alternative and complementary medicines. When one's energy is balanced he/she can balance

Heavenly Text

another's energy by being a vessel for God's energy to flow through them.

There are all kinds of energy work and workers: reiki, massage, reflexology, therapeutic touch, healing touch, sound therapy, acupressure, acupuncture, cranial/sacral therapy, shiatsu, jin shin do, trigger point therapy, quantum touch, matrix energetic, theta healing, and others. No matter what the name or approach, all use energy.

Mankind has always used energy to help balance their bodies. The ancients realized the importance of energy and its healing powers. By stimulating certain energy points the Chinese corrected imbalances in the body to support the health of the body. This is known in the East as acupressure and acupuncture and has been passed down though the ages for at least 5000 years. With practice, over the years, I can now sense and feel these meridians with my fingers.

In the West, the Native American Indians used energy, herbs, dance, and sound. Their medicine was called shamanism. I know we are made of sound and light and use both in my practice. Homeopathic medicine is my preference when the body needs assistance.

So I ask why did the use of energy medicine, for a time, become obsolete? I've read that healings were foremost in the thoughts of Christians until 400 A.D. when Pope Innocent proclaimed and declared "only priests were to heal and to anoint individuals." It was then that mankind turned their healing over to priests instead of taking care of themselves and each other.

Also when our medical forefathers crossed the ocean to the Americas they did not honor the ancient East's contributions to medicine and began a medicine oriented

Heavenly Text
toward diagnosing and treating disease.

I believe our current medical system is failing us in many ways by treating the patient with medicine, surgery, and drugs instead of preventive medicine. This is rapidly changing and energy medicine is becoming more and more accepted.

Because everyone's hands carry an electrical charge, hands can be used to produce movement and align the body's energies and ignite the power, the Light of God within us.

The body is an exquisite unique vibration - an intelligent system of vibrating energy. It has been demonstrated that changing our thoughts from happy to sad instantly creates electrochemical changes in the brain. Manipulating the body with one's hands changes the electrochemical impulses in the body. Just as a radio signal creates physical vibrations that result in sound, changes to an energy system in the body exert a domino effect that modifies the body's chemistry. In this way stress - or disruptions in the body's energy system - eventually causes disease. Properly managing one's energy helps the body stay healthy. Energy medicine is a noninvasive way to benefit the body's energy system.

So what is the body's energy system? The ancients have long known that the body is made of meridians and chakras (the spiritual body) that regulate the body's electrical system. The connective tissue in our body is able to send impulses throughout our body to store energy, filter energy information, and amplify energy to every cell of our body.

Some individuals "sense" this energy. I am known as a sensitive. An individual called a medical intuitive can "see" this spiritual energy in and around the body - the aura. (So far our sophisticated medical equipment cannot see this spiritual energy.) A medical intuitive can see inside the body

Heavenly Text

pinpointing disruptions, help diagnosis problems, and offer suggestions to eliminate or correct the cause. I sense and feel what is going on in another's body. I hear instruction from Spirit, and lay on hands to help restore balance.

Learning to bring your body into better health and balance through energy medicine reinforces the body's systems. I believe this is what Jesus taught us. He used the power of the Holy Spirit to heal. He said, "Lay hands on them and they will heal." Jesus gave us, ALL of US, the message many times to use our hands to heal others. I believe the Holy Spirit is a gift to us all, including priests, as we are all invited by God to use this Spirit power and energy. Jesus came and showed us how to "lay- hands-on- individuals" to heal them by sharing His Energy, His Light, the Power of God, the Holy Spirit. I have learned we can heal others spiritually, mentally, and physically. From illnesses, addictions, and enslavements by being vessels of this healing power.

I know we can all learn to balance our bodies, and our spiritual bodies, and begin to heal from within by using energy medicine. I've been witness to this many times. I have witnessed instant spontaneous healings although most healings are progressive. Progressive healings occur as individuals open to the Divine within. I call the healing work I do Spirit/Energy work. My intention is a huge part of my energy work. One can learn to match one's heart and one's intentions with the intentions of others. It is learning to get out of the way and let the energy of God do the work.

I believe some energy workers feel they are doing the energy work, whereas, others become vessels, opening themselves with intention to the flow of the power of the Holy Spirit and this is when healings occur. When there is acceptance of the outcome with a grateful heart, and no expectations of a reward, the miraculous happens. If we strive

Heavenly Text

to become one with universal consciousness, communications with the heavens opens to us.

For years I wrestled with all my new information trying to combine all with my spiritual background. I am a Catholic. Too often alternative healing work is thought of as New Age and not of God. I became a vessel via an unbelievable journey. The mysteries of the universe have been revealed to me through unsolicited events and encounters, through ordinary and extraordinary experiences. Over the years, I gradually learned to integrate my thoughts. What was confusing became clear. I went through multiple stages of enlightenment. Doubts, challenges and circumstances made little sense to me at times, but were prerequisite for what was to come.

God sought me. Since 1983, my life has witnessed and been filled with ultimate sorrow and ultimate joy. I had to learn that the chaos of this world and my life were but a gift to enable me to grow. God heightened my awareness by involving me in a spiritual education that demanded deep faith for my acceptance. My life changed once I accepted that something beyond me totally governs my actions.

Over a period of years I visited several apparition sites and was blessed with seeing the spirit of Mary, the Mother of Jesus. This taught me the spirit world is real and accessible. I then began to have spiritual visions and prophetic dreams. In time I learned to become an open vessel for the power of God to manifest itself through me. Laying-on-of-hands and other healing modalities became a part of my life. I learned to release past karma, negative energy, and earthbound spirits.

For me, growing in my spirituality has included the whole of all religions, and of all faiths. I believe when all systems of religion are purified of human intervention and dogma, they will be identical, and all will merge back together. It appears to

Heavenly Text

me that it is easier for the many individuals to engage in certain ritual patterns and religions, than to confront God directly. Personal growth and responsibility is our job here on earth. We should always be reaching for higher levels. As our minds and consciousness expand we gradually become who we are meant to be.

I feel Christ's church has been hindered down through the centuries by its almost fanatic zeal to make "Christians of all people" and not "all people followers of Christ." Theological doctrine has been emphasized more than love and understanding. Christ belongs to all of humanity, not to religions of the world. Christ came to show us and teach us the way to salvation. He taught us that death and suffering are part of life and can be overcome. I feel Christianity has overly emphasized the suffering and crucifixion of Jesus instead of examples of how He lived His life. More attention needs to be given to Christ's Lessons of Love, His way of life, His Healings, His Resurrection, and His Ascension, which all brought about His Transfiguration.

Whether it is religion, science, or medicine, I believe we are all looking for the same thing: Peace. We have lost touch with the feminine side of reality, the love of nature, intuition, reverence, intimacy, tenderness - things that some consider sacred. I believe that Mother Mary's visits to the earth are to help us restore these attributes in order to bring about balance. As my soul has evolved, I know from the depths of my being merely talking about faith and spirituality is not enough - we must learn to interact with the Divine.

I am a vessel for the healing power of God. I witness miracles. I see and communicate with the Spirit world. So can you. We all possess the gifts of the Holy Spirit. We just have to learn to use them. I have been fortunate enough to do so. I am neither perfect, nor all knowing. My experiences that stem

Heavenly Text

from God keep me in utter amazement. My life is one of growing and evolving. I have learned to combine the spiritual with the physical and work with the eternal source of all. I am a 69-year-young- woman, who desires to share what I have learned. If I could start learning at age 50, I know anyone can. I speak of what I know as it has been given to me. This wisdom is available for us all if we listen to that still small voice residing deep in our soul. Learning to hear God's messages means entering into a state of awareness, surrendering to the experience, and becoming one in thought with Him. I believe the miraculous is not about science, but is about belief - acceptance without proof. To commune with the heavens, one must be open to all possibilities, believe in the seen and unseen, and be willing to participate in non-reality.

I receive messages in prayer, meditation, prophetic dreams, visions, and experiences throughout each day when encountering a profoundness that demands to be recognized. My once narrow view has expanded into a knowingness I want to share, since I documented over one thousand pages depicting my spiritual evolution. I write from the standpoint of evaluating the benefits for me rather than attempting to prove validity to others. It is my desire my story will enhance others to become aware of their own God Messages (+'s). (Throughout my writings I will type (+) in order not to repeat my favorite phrase, "Must be a God Message".)

We are living in an unprecedented time in history when this gift, this Power, *"Light Energy of God,"* is more prevalent than ever before and is available to all. We can become *"Beings of Light."* We can then heal, and be healed. Knowing and believing in this power is the key to eternal life.

Heavenly Text

Heavenly Text

Wisdom Lessons Begin

As time goes on, many mysteries of my faith are becoming clearer and my convictions are stronger. Spiritual wisdom, spiritual knowledge that comes from above, continues to nurture me. I continue to view my questioning and my appetite for discovery as my destiny. The doors continue to open. I consider that the chaos of this world and my life are but a gift to grow. I believe heaven on earth are those times we accept our fate and are able to celebrate the goodness of life in spite of the sufferings we might have to endure. I believe the inner wisdom that comes from above is available for us all if we but open our hearts and listen to the still, small voice within. The wisdom of the ages is readily available, although at times hard to comprehend because of our narrow view of God's plan. As our minds and consciousness expand we gradually become who we are meant to be -- one with the Light of God.

As we evolve in the grand cycle of the evolution of man, balancing the male and female counterparts, I know from the depths of my being, that each of us needs to not just talk about faith and spirituality, but to learn to interact with the Divine.

Once again the internal promptings of the Lord are gnawing at my insides. I know that I must record my thoughts

Heavenly Text

in order to bring rest to my soul. I will again simply tell my story as it happened to me. God has unfolded before me once again visions, prophetic dreams, and internal messages (+'s) that I can't ignore.

July12, 1998. On this day, M.L. said she saw my deceased daughter Pam dressed in white, sitting by a pond, with light radiating from her hands and feet. + She saw Pam immerse my feet and hands into the pond and water bubbled up. To M.L. this meant spiritual energy was radiating from me, and she wondered if I might possibly have invisible stigmata markings. Then M.L. said she saw Pam holding a cocoon and observed a worm crawling out of it (caterpillar?). She saw Pam place the worm on a page in the Bible. Pam told M.L. to tell me to read Isaiah very closely and digest the word of God. M.L. said she wondered if the symbolism of the worm represented me because I am such a bookworm. I, in turn, was thinking of the beautiful butterfly banner that we hung at Pam's funeral which read "I Am Free." Caterpillars turn into butterflies, don't they? Or was this message about the book I had been writing for God?

I reread the lengthy prophet in Scripture a few days later. I heard Isaiah refer over and over to Abraham, his descendants, and Jacob and His chosen. (Did God want me to learn or know more about descendants?)

I found it intriguing to read, "By all means a people must consult its gods, and, on behalf of the living consult the dead." (Isn't this what M.L. does for me?)

Twice Isaiah used the word "worm." "For I, Yahweh, your God, I am holding you by the right hand; I tell you, 'Do not be afraid.' I will help you. Do not be afraid, Jacob, poor worm, men of Israel I will help you..." (Was God affirming His

Heavenly Text

prophecy to me?)

Again, "Their worm will not die nor their fire go out; they will be loathsome to all mankind." (Is Isaiah speaking of souls who endure forever?)

On September 14, 1998. M.L. and I were together and she informed me she saw Jesus and Pam come to my side. + M.L. saw Pam lay her head on my chest. She said she heard Pam say, "I won't be back like this. I'm not needed like this any more." M.L. remarked, "I wonder what 'not like this' means?" She then saw Pam place a golden key in my heart. Then she saw Pam place a tent over my heart with her name on it and she departed. + We questioned what the symbolism meant. My heart ached realizing M.L. wouldn't be giving me any more messages from Pam. I wondered why this was happening on Pam's birth date. (M.L. did not know that Pam had been born on September 14, 1961. I found it interesting that Pam was leaving on the same date she had originally come into my life.)

After M.L. left I again turned to Isaiah and found, "For, over all, the glory of Yahweh will be a canopy and a tent to give shade by day from the heat, refuge and shelter from the storm and the rain." (What an interesting correlation.)

My mind was questioning. Was the golden key for me to open my heart wider? Was the Isaiah message telling me about the storm to come? I know a tent was used by Moses to receive the word of God. Was God going to be sending me more messages? Were my writings going to continue?

December 8, 1998. (A feast day of Mother Mary.) I had a very unusual dream. + In my dream I was with my daughter Deanna who was nauseated from her pregnancy. (At the time Deanna was pregnant and had been experiencing lots of

Heavenly Text

nausea. She was due the first part of February.) In the dream I suggested to her that I would be happy to carry the baby in my womb for awhile so she could rest. She sighed with relief. She reached between her legs and pulled the baby out and handed it to me. Then I pushed the baby up inside of me. I could feel life inside of me, kicking and moving. I remarked, "I'd forgotten how a baby feels inside." After a short while Deanna remarked, "I really feel bad about this Mom. This doesn't feel right. I think I better take the baby back even though it makes me so sick." I thought to myself, "I sure hope this comes out as easy as it went in." I reached and pulled the baby out between my legs and handed it to her. She replaced the baby into her womb. I remarked, "Wasn't that interesting that we did that without pain." I remembered thinking to myself in my dream, "I thought babies always had a placenta but I guess that's just at birth because this worked so easy."

When I woke up I couldn't get the dream out of my mind. I thought it highly unusual. I called Deanna and shared the dream with her. She replied, "Mom that's the dumbest dream I've ever heard." I agreed, but I was still processing what the dream was conveying to me.

Later, on this afternoon of the 8th, M.L. came to my home. On this occasion, while praying, M.L. said she saw Jesus placing my head in a golden skull cap which came down over my eyes. + She said she thought this meant Spirit would be in control. She could see golden snow flakes surrounding my head. She saw Jesus take a golden snowflake and place it on my heart. + Then she saw the flake dissolve into my heart. Then she saw Jesus getting a table ready for me to write on. She heard that the date March 19 would be a day of silence and a new beginning in my writings. + She remarked, "I hate it when I'm given dates to tell someone."

Heavenly Text

I said, "We'll see what happens, that is months away. I'm now processing the meaning of golden snow flakes - snow can be sparkling, beautiful, and silent."

January 3, 1999. I had an unusual dream about a bird. I've often written my bird stories but this was a bird-dream story. + In my dream I saw something up on a ceiling fan. I reached up and a blue bird flew onto my first finger on my right hand. The bird was the bluest blue I've ever seen. I kept having various dreams all night and always I'd look down and see the blue bird on my finger. Upon waking, I wonder what the bird in my dream was telling me. All I could think was maybe the blue bird was going to help me as I click the mouse using my computer with my right hand. I recalled the phrase, "blue bird of happiness."

January 9, 1999. + I had a prophetic dream of seeing a puzzle being put together. I saw pictures of people and places, shaped liked puzzle pieces coming together. I saw Mother Mary in one of the pieces. I saw Jesus on a cross in one of the pieces. I saw lots of things, but I couldn't remember all of the pictures the next morning. I remembered how the shapes and pieces kept coming together like working a puzzle in mid-air.

I also had another dream that night, that I was in an open field with small children and a tornado came. In the morning I looked up tornado in my dream book: One seeks shelter from a storm by going within. I wonder what is coming? Was the putting together the puzzle going to be part of the storm? Was I to go within and meditate more?

January 12, 1999. M.L. and I were together. She remarked, "This is strange, I see a blue bird on your heart." +

Heavenly Text

She then saw Mother Mary covering us with her blue mantle. I shared my blue bird dream. M.L. sheepishly said "That is too weird, a double message." I answered, "I know I write from my heart and I know Mother Mary helps me."

January 18, 1999. Laverne was in town and did Spirit/energy work on me and remarked at one point, "I see Jesus putting up a fence. It's a deep blue fence around your heart to hold in love. I see a child. Only very special people will ever see this fence." + I pondered on the information. I then shared with her my blue bird dream, and M.L. seeing the blue bird on my heart. (I was intrigued. What is being conveyed to me? Why all these blue messages?)

January 22,1999. Around 4pm a friend was at my home and we were sharing Spirit/energy work. At one point she remarked, "The lower section of your body is so hot. Heat is just radiating from it." I shared that my daughter was in labor and laughingly remarked, "I must be having sympathy pains," then half-jokingly, half-seriously continued, "We truly are all one you know." I explained that the doctor had induced labor and we were anxiously awaiting a call from her husband, Jeff.

Throughout the day Deanna had kept me posted on her progress. At 5:15pm we received a frantic call from Jeff rapidly exclaiming, "Our baby boy was born at 5:08, but something is wrong. The doctor and nurses ran out of the room with him the minute he was born. We are going to name him Justin. Deanna is fine. I'll call you back as soon as I know something." Thus began a long ordeal.

Throughout the next couple of hours we heard from Deanna, who tearfully told us that Justin had been born with a heart problem and they transferred him to Children's Hospital.

Heavenly Text

I feared the worst.

As the night wore on we received more information and learned that Justin had been born with transposition of the great heart vessels. In addition, the hole in his heart was not large enough to transfer his blood from ventricle to ventricle. He had been placed on a respirator and on a ECMO machine (a machine that oxygenated and circulated his blood in his body). They were literally keeping him alive by machines.

Deanna desperately wanted to go to Children's Hospital, but her doctor told her she should wait until morning. Jeff had gone with Justin. We told Deanna we would pick her up and take her to the other hospital. I shed many tears during the next hours knowing the agony Deanna and Jeff must be experiencing, that we were all experiencing.

After a restless night we left for St. Louis, approximately two hours away. When we were nearing St. Louis I spotted a hawk in a tree by the side of the road and secretly whispered, "Thanks, are you here to help?" I don't how to explain it but it felt like it was there for me. In times of trouble, I'm always sent help and this seemed to be Spirit's way of saying +"I am with you."

Deanna had told us the doctor said she could leave about 9am. My heart was breaking when I entered her room and saw the sorrow in her eyes and heard the anxiousness in her voice. She was doing amazingly well considering she had just delivered a baby a little over twelve hours ago. She said she had not slept all night. She and Jeff had talked on the phone often. Justin was soon to be taken to surgery for the delicate operation of enlarging the hole in his heart. She desperately wanted to see her baby. She briefly saw him at delivery and hoped she would get to see him before the surgery began.

When we arrived at Barnes Children's Hospital, we

encountered an exhausted Jeff. Deanna joined Jeff in the intensive care unit to see their baby hooked up to an array of equipment. I cannot imagine the pain of the moment.

Then the doctor briefed all of us on the seriousness of the surgery to enlarge the hole in his heart and explained that it was the first in of a series of many. He also explained how Justin's problem originated at about six weeks in the womb. He said that it is impossible for an ultra-sound to detect the problem. Statistics show that babies born with this problem are about one in every two thousand births.

Throughout the morning Jeff's parents and other members of his family, who live in St. Louis, arrived. We all gathered in a waiting room during surgery. Deanna sat with the rest of us, in a chair on a pillow with hurting stitches. It was a terribly long day. Finally, about eight hours later, a sigh of relief when the doctor came in and said Justin had survived the surgery. The doctor still painted a very grim picture. He explained that if Justin's heart recovered enough they would perform the delicate surgery of reversing the great heart vessels in a few days. They would have to take each day one at a time. He let us all know how critical the situation was and I detected little hope in his voice.

Deanna and Jeff then spent a few minutes at Justin's side in intensive care. Shortly thereafter we took an exhausted daughter to her home for a much needed rest. Jeff remained at the hospital. When we arrived at their home, some friends had cleaned their house, the first of many kind gestures we witnessed from their friends. A family member brought home her five-year-old daughter, Kristine.

Kristine wanted me to sleep with her in her room. I was in her bed, she on the floor in a sleeping bag for a few short minutes when she whispered, "Danny, (her endearing name for

Heavenly Text

me) can I get in bed with you?" Naturally, I agreed. I spent a restless night in a twin bed with Kristine, who slept deeply at my side. Erv was on the couch in the basement. I presumed Deanna was feeling restless, helpless, and alone in her own bed. I wondered often if anyone was sleeping. I knew I wasn't.

During the night as I prayed I had a profound happening that I didn't understand. I kept telling God that I wanted whatever was His will concerning Justin. I asked over and over to give Deanna some rest, to let her feel His presence, and to be with us all. I kept remembering how I felt the first day we discovered Pam had leukemia. I knew some of what Deanna must be feeling although I know each person's sorrow is for them alone. My heart was breaking. I remember praying, "God how should I pray? I don't even know if it is best for Justin to live. Will his body be okay? Will his brain be okay? Would it be best for him to die? Is there anything I can do? Are you going to use me as a vessel of your healing power?" Then I distinctly heard, +*"Nancy, You must ask if you want to help Justin. Ask if you want to be part of his life."* I pleaded with deep sincerity, "God, if you can use me to help in anyway, I am yours." Instantly, I had a terrific pain pass through the right side of my heart. I thought at first I was having a heart attack. Then it subsided. + I had a deep sense of knowing that I was part of something big, but I knew not what. I wondered what had taken place. I continued to pray.

At dawn Deanna came into Kristine's room and said, "Mom, I want to go to the hospital. I can't stand not being there. I was awake most of the night talking to God. I need to go." We shared a few heartfelt moments and I went to wake Erv who was already awake. We left for the hospital, dropping Kristine off at her other grandparents.

Heavenly Text

Deanna and Jeff remained at Justin's bedside in intensive care almost constantly. Sometime during the day the grandparents were permitted to go in to see him. We took our ten minute turns. Seeing that precious little angel with tubes everywhere and Deanna sitting by the side of his bed holding his little hand was very disturbing to say the least. We, Erv and I, laid hands on Justin and prayed. I didn't feel the usual sensations that I normally feel when laying on of hands. I cried and seemed to only shake inside. I was upset with myself after I left, and wondered why I couldn't seem to get a better grip. Yet I knew this was different because I too was emotionally involved and exhausted. I felt God wasn't using me as his vessel but was using me in a different way that I couldn't explain.

We again spent the night at Deanna's home. The next day, when we returned to the hospital and had our turn to go in to intensive care, I prayed to remain calm and for God to use me as he saw fit. As I held Justin's little feet (the only part of him not wired up) I had a profound Spirit/energy sensation that words cannot describe. As the surge went through me, I felt as if I was going to fall over, and my feet began to burn with a tremendous heat. I heard within very clearly, + *"Re-birthing, re-birthing."* I said nothing, but thought to myself, "I sure made a connection this time. God, what is going on? What does re-birthing mean?" Erv and I stayed for only a short time longer. As we left I found it difficult to walk out as my feet felt on fire. I still said nothing, as I knew all present would think I was crazy. I knew God was at work in a big way, but I did not understand. I thought to myself, "In time I guess I'll understand all of this."

After lunch, Kristine was also allowed to see Justin for a short while. I wondered what was going on in her little mind.

Heavenly Text

We all spent time during the day trying to decide what to do next, how to help, knowing there was really nothing anyone could do but wait. We, Erv and I, finally decided to go home to Columbia in order for me to get my car and more clothes, and to return to stay at their house with Kristine the following week. Deanna and Jeff decided to stay around the clock at the hospital. For the time being, Kristine would go to Jeff's parents in St. Louis until I returned.

As Erv and I drove the two hours home I knew in my heart this drive was going to be occurring on an on-going basis for quite some time.

I returned the next day to St. Louis. As I neared St. Louis, I again spotted a hawk in the exact same tree that I had noticed on our first trip. + I prayed a thank you and made a quick short trip to the hospital. Again I felt physical pain in my heart when near Justin.

I then went to Deanna's home to wait for Kristine to return from kindergarten. I stayed most of the week, trying to be of some help, watching Kristine, cooking, washing clothes, and answering many phone calls. Kristine often entertained me. One evening we were playing dolls and I asked, from one doll in my hand to the doll in her hand, "What do you think heaven is like?" The other doll that was held in Kristine's hand answered abruptly, "Why did you ask that?" I said, "I just thought you might know." Kristine then got up with her doll in her hand and began to swing around the room. With her arms outstretched like an angel she was swaying, singing, and proclaiming, "Heaven is all sparkling and pretty. Jesus lives there. Angels are there." + (Words from the mouth of a babe. I felt I had been taken to heaven in that moment. I knew Kristine was probably going to be handling this better than anyone else.)

Some time during the first few days, Justin's lungs collapsed and the prognosis was not good. The machines were literally keeping him alive; without it, he could not breathe. It had been a long week. Another surgery was required to repair leakage of blood in his heart which had resulted from the first surgery. I actually felt the pain although I wasn't there. I wondered what was going on. Why this deep connection? In time his lungs again responded and the doctors decided on a day to perform the major surgery of the transposition of the great heart vessels.

Not wanting Kristine to feel left out, Deanna and Jeff eventually decided on a routine of periodically alternating their visits. A schedule was set up for various family members of Jeff's family to watch Kristine, and by the end of week I returned home.

January 29, 1999. I came home from St. Louis exhausted after that first week of staying with Kristine. I wrote in my journal:

>Here I am Lord. My heart is breaking for Deanna. She had such a difficult pregnancy. . .and now this. I lost a baby at five months and know that deep pain. I had a grown daughter die and know that deep pain. Although I know suffering can bring incredible growth, I hate to see Deanna suffer through this sorrow with her child. I hate for all of us to have to go through pain and sorrow again. I wonder if Pam is with us, but I'm sure she is. I wonder if Justin will remain with us. Why, Why, Why is all of this happening? How can I help? Can you use me as a vessel of your healing power to help Justin, to help Deanna? I'm yours. Tell me what to do. Please answer my "whys." I need your guidance. Thanks, Father in heaven for

Heavenly Text

keeping Justin here with us so far. If Justin lives, I pray for a healthy and happy little boy - fully recovered. Then I suddenly was interrupted and heard, + *"My child, I'm at your side. I told you many will die. I'll take them quickly. Justin is still with you. He is a servant of mine. His job is important. No matter how short or how long. I walk by your side. My love goes out to all who are put on machines to have life."*

I interrupted with, "Should we be using life-saving machines? Are we taking away Your work? Your creation? Interfering with Your will? Help me Lord to understand Your will in this situation."

I then internally heard, + *"Read, Abraham and Isaac."*

As I reread how Abraham gave his son back to God, I thought of how I gave my daughter back to God. I questioned whether Deanna was going to be giving her son back to God. I read, "I swear by my own self, it is Yahweh who speaks, because you have done this, because you have not refused me your son, your only son, I will shower blessings on you. I will make your descendants as many as the stars of heaven and the grains of the sand on the seashore. Your descendants shall gain possession of the gates of their enemies. All of the nations of the earth shall bless themselves by your descendants, as a reward of your obedience." (Genesis 22:15-18)

I also read: "I will create a race from Jacob, and heirs to my mountain from Judah. My chosen shall inherit them, my servants live in them." Isaiah

I couldn't help but think of the words Jesus had said to me concerning Justin, +*"He is my servant."* I wondered, are the descendants of Abraham still coming to this earth? Are they new souls or old souls in new bodies?

That evening Ana invited me to come over and she

Heavenly Text

administered Spirit/energy work on me. I knew I really needed the angels to work on me through her hands. I was tired and worn out physically and emotionally. She laid her hands on me and immediately exclaimed, "This is so unusual. With my eyes closed all I see is this deep blue. I think it has to do with Justin." I told her about my blue bird dream, and Laverne and M.L.'s blue messages. We talked about Justin and how medically he would be called a "blue baby." I shared with her how I was always feeling pain in my body at the same time Justin's body was having difficulty. I decided that the arrival of the blue bird in my life was to remind me to hold happiness in my heart even though times were tough. Was I going to be writing about this? We talked of the many +'s and wondered what it all meant.

A few days later, Erv and I went back to be present for the next surgery, the major surgery of the transposition of the great heart vessels. We had all been informed there was a fifty-fifty chance Justin would not survive the surgery. Again, we all gathered in the waiting room for twelve anxious hours. Again, I felt physical pain in my heart. (Thoughts went through my mind of long-distance healings.) Finally, a somber, exhausted-looking doctor appeared to inform us that Justin had survived the surgery and that he was off the ECMO machine; extremely critical, but alive. The doctor said he had left Justin's chest open to observe his heart. The next twenty-four hours were going to be very, very, critical.

Jeff and Deanna again decided to stay at the hospital. Erv and I went back to their house. During the night, around two in the morning, I was awakened with my heart beating rapidly, actually pounding. I thought for sure I was again having an actual heart attack. I silently lay praying, for two or three hours, wondering if this was me or was something happening

Heavenly Text

to Justin. Deanna called around six in the morning and said, "We almost lost Justin last night around two. They had to resuscitate him and put him back on ECMO" + I said nothing to her of my experience but told Erv, "For some reason I appear to be closely connected to Justin and I keep feeling what is happening in his body. I'm intrigued and very curious. I wonder what God is teaching me."

As long as Justin's chest was open no one but Deanna and Jeff were allowed in the intensive care unit. Fear of infection was great. I can't imagine how hard it must have been to observe him with his exposed heart. (Thoughts of the Exposed Sacred Heart of Jesus entered my mind.) We returned home.

Deanna and I talked on the phone daily, often many times during the day. I received many reports both good and bad. Justin appeared to go steps forward and steps backwards. And throughout the days I was often awakened at night, at different internals, with chest pains. Always the next day Deanna would be confirming the times for me by explaining problems Justin had encountered at those times. I never shared with her what I was feeling or what was going on. I kept praying and wondering if God was using me to heal Justin, but it felt different. As strange as it sounds, I felt Justin was teaching me. Also, many times during the days I would experience odd sensations and would think, "It must be Justin." I spent a lot of time praying and trying to send him love and prayers of comfort and healing.

The doctor had initially informed us that Justin could not be left on the E.C.M.O. machine more than three weeks. As the time neared, the anticipation became intense. It took almost a week to slowly remove him from the machine. We were all elated when he was totally off.

Heavenly Text

Justin was finally on his own, but there was a downside. They had to start giving him a new medication, a very strong medication, which could be hard on his kidneys. He remained on the respirator, plus many, many, other intricate wirings to monitor his body. In a few days his kidneys began to fail and they had to start perennial dialysis on him. There was always something going on, bad days with serious infections, to good up-beat days with good reports. Constant ups and downs.

February 13, 1999. I was awakened in the morning by seeing lots of Light with my eyes closed. Then I saw clearly the face of Mary, the Mother of God. + I uttered, "Thanks, God why now?" Then I remembered it was the 13th, Mary's special day. I knew Mary was letting me know she was watching over me through the difficult times of seeing my daughter experience the pain of giving a child back to God. I knew she understood. (Her heart had been pierced because of her deep love for Christ. Was that it? Was God showing me when we love each other deeply we are connected to them.) I think Mary was also giving me extra courage for the information that was going to be relayed to me.

Later that day, when at my computer writing I wondered what was happening because the energy seemed intense. My heart started beating fast. As the pace of my heartbeat picked up, beating faster and faster, I began to shake and quiver. Then I heard very clearly, + *"Nancy, the time is near. We will begin soon. Be not afraid. You will work with Me. It is important that you tell Father Charlie the new pastor at Newman who took Fr. Mike's place to read your work. He must read it. Tell him I said so. We will begin again soon. Justin is watched over by Me. I love You."*

I replied with, "No way. I can't do that. How can I go in

Heavenly Text

and tell a priest who doesn't understand how I get messages that You said 'he must read my writings?'' I nervously twirled the information around in my mind all that day. I was missing Father Mike.

The next day as I drove to church, I prayed all the way, asking for strength and courage as I confided with God, "If Fr. Charlie is in his office, I will try." When I arrived, not only was Charlie in his office, he was standing in the doorway. I asked if I could come in. Then I sheepishly asked if I could shut the door. He said, "This must be serious." I told him I was shaking inside because I was scared to tell him that I had received a message for him from Jesus. I finally, somehow, feeling like a fool spit out the words, telling him what I heard. He gently said, "Well, I guess I'll have to do that then." I breathed a sigh of relief and left my manuscript, not knowing if he believed a word I said.

(I wondered why Fr. Charlie had suddenly been asked to join the circle?)

February 19,1999. I had a vision. + I saw very clearly a Mongolian looking individual. The face kept getting close and closer. I heard + *"This is your new guide. Vidas."* I responded with, "Thanks God. I'm thrilled to have a new additional guardian angel."

(Later I talked with a Latin student who told me, Vidas, as a proper noun would mean 'protector'. "Double thanks, God. I sure love that message and do I ever need it now.")

February 20, 1999. I had another dream of children and a tornado. Then I woke up. I knew I was presently in the midst of experiencing the storm of sorrow in my life seeing my daughter sorrowing over Justin. I recalled my previous tornado

Heavenly Text
dream. I knew Spirit had previously warned me ahead of time about the difficult experiences we were now going through.

February 25, 1999. M.L. and I got together at her home to pray for Justin. She had purchased a tiny indigo blue bird and gave it to me as a gift saying, "When on vacation I walked into a gift shop and all the way across the room this deep blue color caught my eye. I went to the shelf. I saw it was a blue bird, and immediately, + I knew I was to give it to you because of your blue bird experiences."

We then began to pray and M.L. said she saw Jesus removing 13 barnacles from the left side of my heart. As He lifted them there was a pearl underneath each one. She was told to tell me to read Exodus 28 & 29.

I obeyed. Chapter 28 is the scripture giving explicit directions for the making of priest's vestments for Aaron and his sons, for their consecration to the priesthood. Chapter 29 is about the preparation, consecration, clothing, anointing and offerings for Aaron and his sons. The directions were given for the sacrifice of the rams, the spreading of the blood on Aaron, his son, the ground, and the altar. Then the placing of the lambs on the altar from generation to generation was explained. Yahweh goes on to say that He will remain with the sons of Israel.

Were Pam and Justin the lambs being sacrificed from this generation? Why? I wondered if the thirteen barnacles could represent thirteen generations? I was confused but I continued to process my many thoughts.

When I arrived home I placed the crystal blue bird next to Justin's picture, along with the twenty-four hour candle I had been burning in his honor. This little altar was where I knelt daily and prayed for him.

Heavenly Text

After several weeks they closed Justin's chest with another surgery. Then we were all again able to go back into intensive care to see him. We went back to St. Louis. Justin looked like an angel so helplessly laying there all wired up, with his little finger still grasping Deanna's little finger. Deanna said at times he would squeeze it. Our visit was short but meaningful. Seeing Deanna and Jeff so exhausted and worn out tore at my insides, yet hearing and seeing all their church community and what their friends were doing for them refreshed me. I remember vividly how much strength others gave me when Pam was dying. I thanked God often for their support from others.

February 26, 1999. The day of a **jolting** meditation. In the early morning while meditating I suddenly had a profound and startling realization, a mind quickening, a spiritual knowing, whatever one wants to call it, entered my awareness. I heard, +*"Your daughter/son lives."* I questioned in disbelief, "What are you telling me? That Justin is going to die. I was overwhelmed with emotion. A strange awareness entered my consciousness. I knew Spirit was telling me Justin was going to die but that he and Pam still lived. My body shook as tears flowed from my eyes. But I felt like I was being told they were one and the same. "Why are you telling me this now?" + I then saw before me the events of the last few months as I was reminded of. . .the profound dream of Deanna's baby in my body. . .the feelings in my uterus the night Justin was born. . .why I'd been so connected physically feeling his pain in my body. . .why I had a dream years ago of a baby on my shoulder. . .why I kept hearing re-birthing, re-birthing when I touched Justin's feet. . .why I had the experiences with the blue bird. . .why I was told to read Abraham and Isaac. . .why M.L. had

Heavenly Text

said, "Pam won't be here 'like this' anymore". . .other dreams. . .my first book beginning with Pam dying. . .and now this? Are you trying to explain to me how we are all connected, so intertwined that what happens to one happens to another? Then I thought of the dream of the puzzle pieces coming together.

Then I heard, +*"I rejoice with you that you have figured out the puzzle. Rejoice in your joy today. Go forth and know that I love you. We will begin to write again soon."*

I was so shaken I must have cried for an hour. I reviewed my dreams, my visions, the recent message I'd received and tried to piece it all together. Memories flooded my mind of past experiences. Was God telling me I was going to be writing about oneness and spiritual evolution and generational healing. I said, "I don't know if I can do that." I heard, +*"You should never be ashamed of witnessing for the Lord."* (Timothy:8)

Then one day Deanna called with the news that the doctors felt there was no hope left because Justin's kidneys had totally stopped functioning. The doctors, along with Deanna and Jeff, had decided to discontinue all procedures and let Justin die. I'm sure an extremely painful moment for them. (I recalled my jolting meditation.) The doctor told them that he thought once procedures were stopped that Justin would die within twenty four hours. Deanna and Jeff were allowed to hold him for the first time. I can't imagine how painful it had been for Deanna not to be able to fulfill this motherly need. Deanna then went on to say, "If you want to hold him Mom you need to come up today." The timing was impossible, but I told her if Justin was still alive we would come the next day.

Erv was unable to go to St. Louis the next day because of a previous serious commitment so I called my son Joe. He said he had been thinking about going, so Joe and I decided to go

Heavenly Text

together. When we arrived in the morning the decision had again been made for no one to hold Justin. This time the decision was made by Deanna and Jeff who were still worrying about infection. I knew in my heart they were scared, still longing for a miracle cure, but weren't we all? I was hurt, sorry that I didn't get to hold him, but said nothing. I knew I had to honor their feelings and let them do what made them feel best. Justin was terribly swollen because of non-functioning kidneys. Yet, he appeared to be very restful. Joe and I visited for a short while, surrounded Justin, Deanna, and Jeff with our love and came home.

Deanna again called two days later and said "I'm sorry you didn't get to hold Justin when you were here, but now you can if you want to come up again. We want to take a picture with each grandparent holding him." Erv and I went in the next day.

March 19, 1999. For me, it was the third, two hundred and fifty mile round-trip, in six days. When we got there Deanna and Jeff were waiting. They suggested Erv hold him first. Erv held Justin for about twenty minutes and Jeff took a few pictures. As I sat there, seeing all of the wires and monitors still attached to him, resting in Erv's arms, I couldn't help but shed silent tears inside.

When I took Justin in my arms, Deanna, Jeff, and Erv decided to go to breakfast. I held Justin for about an hour praying, sending special messages to heaven, trying to share a lifetime of love. My mind was in a turmoil as I relived all that had been transpiring. Thinking of my jolting meditation. Thinking of Pam being born. Thinking of Pam dying. Talking to Justin. Talking to Pam.

I wanted God's will, whatever it would be, to be done. I would have loved to have seen Justin healed but that was

Heavenly Text

looking very unlikely. I was dealing with a lot of emotional private thoughts. I knew deep inside Justin would be leaving us soon. He was a tough little guy and had surprised all of the doctors and care givers that he had lasted throughout the week. Doctors had been baffled that he had lived so long. I felt the human touch was what kept him alive for the extended days.

I whispered to him, "Did you live this entire week so I would be able to hold you, so I could say a private goodbye?" As tears streamed down my face I shared all of my troubled thoughts with God, with Pam and Justin, asking over and over, "Why? Why? Why?" Although as I held Justin, I felt an unbelievable presence come over me of peace, comfort, and joy that I cannot explain. + No one will ever know how the moments affected me. I was alone in my thoughts because I had not told any one of my ongoing experiences, and I was thinking I never would. I considered holding my grandchild a special, special, spiritual encounter, of holding a real angel in my arms. +

(Was I, Pam, Deanna, Justin being used in some mysterious way for generational healing? Justin had taught me how to give more of myself. This entire experience had definitely taught me how "totally" connected we all are. We truly are all one.)

While at breakfast Erv asked Deanna and Jeff if they minded if he made a casket for Justin. Erv told me he had asked them stating, "If there would be a miracle and he lives then he could use it for a toy box in the future." They seemed pleased and told him they thought that would be special.

When we got home Erv went to the funeral home to get the dimensions of an infant's casket. He then purchased the amount of oak wood needed. The first thing the next morning he began making Justin's casket and finished it about three

Heavenly Text

o'clock in the afternoon. I was impressed with the workmanship. I think Erv surprised himself in how well it turned out.

About 3:30pm on that day, March 20, 1999, we received word Justin had died. At last the long painful ordeal had culminated. I prayed, "Dear God, I know you have a new angel in heaven. Please give Deanna and Jeff more strength to get through the next few days. Give us all strength."

I immediately got in the car and went to purchase some white satin to line the casket. Later, Joe and Kathy came over, and we surprised ourselves by easily lining the wooden box. It looked professionally done.

When Deanna and Jeff went to the funeral home to make arrangements, the director told them to make whatever arrangement they wanted and informed them their church had already paid for everything. Knowing how much friends and family had done for them, they decided to have Justin laid out for several hours for visitation. Deanna said to me, "It'll give everyone closure. Besides, the family has only seen him on machines and wired up." Deanna and Jeff decided to leave the casket open for the first thirty minutes, just for immediate family.

That night I had a very clear vision. I saw three circles of light and saw shadows of people in these circles. I heard very clearly, + "*Your soul group is becoming one. You are coming back to you.*" I questioned, "What is a soul group?" I was mystified and confused. I wondered, "Is this telling me Pam and Justin are an aspect of me? Who else am I part of?" I felt this vision was an affirmation of my startling meditation, yet I remained very confused.

I prayed and pleaded, "Thanks, God, I'm lost here. Please help me. What am I supposed to do with all of this

Heavenly Text
information? Help me. Help me."

The next day I began looking everywhere for information on soul groups, for books on rebirth, on anything that might help to pull my thoughts together. I read multiple authors on the subject and started gathering multiple ideas that cannot be proven by anyone.

I read *Science of the Vortex* by David Ash which helped: "Life can be portrayed as the one-self, one form of super energy, existing as the collective of an infinite number of selves, fanning out into a network below. An analogy would be like an octopus floating on the surface of the ocean with its tentacles outstretched. At the end of each tentacle is another octopus connecting to yet more octopi. A signal from any tentacle of any octopus would affect the others."

For me this matched the parable Jesus gave us, "I'm the vine, you are the branches." So I finally decided the series of occurrences were God's way of simply trying to help me better understand how we are all connected, how we are one. I often feel in my body what is going on in others but this time the intensity had been somewhat different--ongoing. I know there are all kinds of healings--heart, mind, body, and soul--and I believe this one must have been of my soul. Knowing of this truth was my healing. (Wouldn't the world be a different place if each of us treated others as though they were part of ourselves? Thanks, God.)

March 23, 1999. We got to St. Louis early and brought the casket to the funeral home. When family arrived for viewing, Kristine was so excited. She was getting to show off her baby brother and proudly announced, "This is my brother Justin, but he's not really here. He is in heaven with Jesus."

Heavenly Text

She said it with such conviction that I believe she understood more than anyone present.

The funeral home was packed for hours. The next morning there was a church service, and then the burial at the cemetery. Believe it or not, there is a cemetery in St. Louis which gives a free plot to families who lose a child at birth. All of these kindnesses made my heart rejoice because we seldom hear of the good other people do. Deanna and Jeff had been showered with love.

It had been a long two months but closure was brought to many. Our immediate family will always feel the loss of little Justin. I know the loss will be hardest on Deanna and Jeff, but I also know time heals. I know, from my personal experiences, that sorrow and pain can create growth. I pray this will be the case for all of us.

I must add here that every trip I made back and forth to St. Louis I had always spotted a hawk, in the same tree, as I neared St. Louis. On our return trip home after the funeral I received a special gift from the heavens. As we neared Columbia, I spotted two hawks, side by side, on a tree branch. + It was very special and I locked the memory in my heart. ("Thanks, God.")

I prayed, "Jesus, I pray for Deanna whose heart was broken by the loss of her son. Please be with her in a special way. She has been through so many tragedies with her three accidents, her dozen or more surgeries, (*Heavenly Text* Vol. I), and now the death of her son. Someday I'll tell her how Justin expanded my mind. I pray someday she'll be ready to comprehend. I know I understand better how, in our darkest hours, we are never alone, and that our loved ones are with us often in ways we don't totally understand. I wonder if this experience of losing Justin will start Deanna on the road of

Heavenly Text

soul searching as Pam's death did for me? I know that earth is a school for our souls and that we learn from every experience. I know as parents when a soul chooses to come to us, it is a gift. I also believe if one doesn't discover the gift of that soul and learn the lessons it came to teach, the gift is lost. To deny the purpose of anything is to deny the reasons for life. I do know, in the long run, all that has touched Deanna will greatly enhance her life in some way. In my heart of hearts, I know she's destined for something great. I wonder what You have in mind for her? Bless her, Jesus; bless us all."

Then that night I had a nightmare, which is very unusual for me. I was being held in the corner of a room by two people who had big boards or sticks in their hands. I knew they were going to beat me. I woke up shaking.

Why would I feel up against a wall? I wondered what my future held.

March 27, 1999. I had a dream in which I could see a very high mountain. Then the top came off and exploded and I realized I was viewing a volcano. Lava came very close to where I was. End of dream.

Then I had a second dream. This dream was about a conservation program that had trees to be adopted. I picked out a tree to adopt with just a trunk, no branches, no leaves. Erv thought it was a ridiculous choice. But as I got closer to the tree and looked closely, I could see the tree had little green pimple protrusions which were trying to become branches. +

As I thought about these two dreams I felt the volcano certainly represented me as I am trying to process all the explosive thoughts that were being revealed to me. Had the lava burned the branches off the tree? Did the tree represent

Heavenly Text

me now feeling naked and alone? I wanted my branches to grow but I knew I needed to live by God's time. I had to remind myself that often we forget we wait for growth. It is in silence and waiting that something grand can happen. This is when one's authentic being comes to life.

I prayed, "It seems to me God, that I'm waiting for so many things. Be with me as I process all of this."

March 29, 1999. I prayed and talked to God while journaling. I wrote: I guess it's time for me to get clearer what it is You want me to know and do. You never cease to amaze me. As I try to put the pieces together please whisper in my ear and help me to understand better. Have my experiences these past months been about generational healing? I now better understand why I felt in my body what was going on in Justin's body, the oneness, the connection. I prayed daily for a miracle healing for Justin, yet now he has died. He's gone back home. I know his mission was great, that he has affected many and taught many lessons to us all. Help me to understand better... I suddenly heard, + *"My child you are always worried and want to understand all. Let it be. Time will take care of your concerns. I give you strength and courage to go on--to work for Me. Continue to reach out to others with love and kindness. Watch My children come to you in love and hope. Fill them with peace. I will continue to fill your mind with thoughts to help make sense of My plan. Let go and return to Me as my secretary and we will reach out to multitudes. My arms surround you. Clear your mind and heart. Prepare for clearing of your soul. Work diligently for My purpose and My work will be accomplished. Smile through your eyes for the world to see Me in you."*

Heavenly Text

April 1,1999. M.L. and I were praying together and she said she could see my heart. She described it as a very rich pink, with two cords coming from it. She said, + "I think it has to do with Pam and Justin, but I don't understand." She kept seeing the cords throughout our time together. (Inside I kept smiling to myself and wondering, "Could these cords be representing their lives? Does this have anything to do with soul groups? ")

M.L. then saw Jesus removing some scars of emotion off the right side of my heart. + In my mind I thought of the first night Justin was born and experiencing actual pain in the right side of my heart. I said nothing.

After M.L. left my mind could not rest. Was this an affirmation? The two cords in my heart certainly seemed to indicate that Pam and Justin were aspects of me. I remembered M.L. previously telling me she saw Jesus removing 13 barnacles from the left side of my heart. I thought even more about generational healing--this lifetime and other lifetimes?

April 19,1999. M.L. was again praying with me. As she laid her hands on my face she relayed, + "Your eyes will see within. Your ears will hear." Then she said she saw Jesus washing me with the blood of the lamb. As she uttered those words I literally felt a physical sensation go through my body. It was like a lightning strike and I shook all over. + M.L. and I were both startled. I remembered previously reading the scripture from Exodus and the anointing of Aaron and his sons for the priesthood. Then M.L. said she saw Jesus baptizing me with eternal water. Again I felt a strong lightning strike and I shook all over. + The moment was very intense for both of us. As I felt the sensations in my body I saw a bright light and I knew in my heart that I was receiving an abundance of graces.

Heavenly Text

I questioned silently to myself, "For what, God? To write all I've witnessed? Was the lightning strike a jolt to open my heart wider? My mind? Thanks, for Your abundance of love and graces. I'm trying to collect my thoughts and be strong."

Afterward I again went to Isaiah. Under the heading of the mission of the prophet I read: "The Lord Yahweh has given me a disciple's tongue. So that I may know how to reply to the wearied He provides me with speech. Each morning He wakes me to hear, to listen like a disciple. The Lord Yahweh has opened my ear." (Isaiah 50:4)

"I am coming to gather the nations of every language...And some of them I will make priest..."(Isaiah 66:18-22)

Are You asking me to again write what I see and hear? Are You telling me we are all priests in Your priesthood? The priests of Melchizedek? I recalled my other ear experiences at Helen's, at Caritas, when the statue arrived, and on and on. Was this experience a new signal to write?

May 6, 1999. Sometime during the night while laying awake I saw a living eye, very clearly, for a lengthy time. + I kept thanking God again for His gifts. I kept pleading, "What are You trying to tell me? What is the purpose? Please give me the graces for understanding the mission You want me to do."

May 15, 1999. + I had a vision of seeing a table. Then a book appeared on the table. I could see a pair of reading glasses. Someone in a white robe picked up the glasses and walked away. I saw sandals on the feet as the white robe walked away. I heard, *"Can You walk with me the whole way?"* (Matt 11:24)

Heavenly Text

I prayed, "I've got the message Lord. You're telling me to write. You keep giving me the message clearer and clearer. I'll try. It'll be so hard but I promise I'll start again soon. I believe You are telling me that if I don't start writing, You will have to get someone else to write for You."

May 16, 1999. + I dreamed that Anne (my teacher and mentor) was here in Missouri, doing Spirit/energy work on many people. She took a break and went outside. I followed her outside. We were talking when a woman holding a child in her arms came over to us. The child was crying. Anne took the child in her arms and began to nurse it. I remember thinking, "She'll do anything for anybody." Shortly the child calmed down. Then the child turned towards me and reached out its hand and touched my face. + I commented to the child, "What power I feel. Your hands are so powerful." Anne said, "Yes, now He knows us both. You will be able to help Him when I leave."

When I woke up I was in a state of awe and delight. "Thank You, thank You," was running through my mind even though I wasn't sure of the entire significance of the spiritual dream. I felt peaceful and was full of joy. I felt in my heart that the symbol of the woman with child was Mary, holding the baby Jesus.

I wondered if Jesus was using Anne in my dream to give me confirmation that I indeed do have the gift of being a vessel for healings, and I would be working with Him more deeply. (I silently questioned and prayed, "Was this a kind of graduation? Does this mean teaching others as Anne does? Will I be working in a more pronounced way? But I still feel like a child learning Your healing work.")

I know breast has to do with a mother's nourishment and

Heavenly Text

love. I thought, "This is what I do in my Spirit/energy work -- give nourishment and love. This is what Anne does. She has taught me as well. We give of ourselves." Was Jesus passing His blessing on to me to help others?

I was excited about the dream and called Anne. I was shocked to discover she had had a mystical experience that same morning. When I relayed my dream to her she immediately responded, "Nancy, that is a very powerful dream. I think God is up to something here. Guess what happened to me this morning? Something that has never happened before. When taking a shower I noticed blood coming from the nipple of my breast. I silently called upon God for the meaning and was informed that it was nothing to worry about...that it was a sign of His blood. + I heard the word stigmata."

I was stunned. + We both were struck with the unusual synchronicity of the two occurrences. A two-way message. A first. We knew it was a huge " +." But what?

I was elated with the realization that my dream was authenticated by Spirit through Anne's experience. Being with Anne has always been like attending God's own party, a continuous celebration of the mysteries of life, of growth and change. She has nurtured me with nourishment and love over the years. She always gives of her entire being. She awakens in me thoughts I didn't know exist. She stretches my mind. She has led me into self discovery. I've always wondered if I could ever remotely measure up to her. Now my dream seemed to be saying that I could.

After our conversation I looked up blood in the dream book. (Blood: to give blood means to engage one's emotions, to give of one's self from the deep core of one's being. Blood is a symbol of spiritual rebirth.)

Hadn't I given of my flesh and blood by giving Pam back

Heavenly Text

to God? Hadn't Deanna given of her flesh and blood by giving Justin back to God? I had shared my deep love with Justin and Pam; and isn't life suppose to be all about love? Could the giving of my physical self for Justin have been a rebirthing of sorts for me? I had heard "rebirthing." I knew that a stigmata means a person manifests the wounds of Christ's crucifixion. I know that stigmata is a spiritual mystery passed down through the ages. I think of St. Francis of Assisi of long ago and Padre Pio of modern times. I realize there are many individuals who carry this mark of Christ. Recently, I heard or read somewhere that there is believed to be about three hundred persons marked with the stigmata in the world at this time. Was Jesus letting me know how He works within us? How the blood of Christ is still alive in the world? How we are to give of ourselves, our blood? I recalled the experience with M.L. and the baptizing experience and her relaying the message of an invisible stigmata.

I prayed, "Thanks, Jesus for the powerful dream message. Was this my spiritual rebirth? Was this a healing? Is this what individuals call Christ Consciousness? I do know it was You passing on Your love and strength, and probably the stigmata sign was just to let me know the gift was from You. My heart swells with joy. Thank You for Your blessing. Thank You again for bringing Anne into my life. Thank You for the affirmation on how we can pass on to others what we know ourselves by just giving of ourselves. A healing did take place. I will start to write again for You. I know You want me to write ALL that I experienced."

May 19, 1999. For several weeks I had been constantly seeing the living eye. + It had taken me a couple of months to decide if I was to write about my experiences with Justin. The

Heavenly Text

task was very challenging. I finally had decided to obey. I went to my computer and began writing this chapter.

It was much later that I remembered M.L. had given me the message on December 8, 1998, that I would begin to write on March 19. Justin died on March 20th. December 8, 1998, is also the date of the unusual dream I had of transferring the baby from Deanna's womb to mine. Very interesting! Was that dream telling me Deanna was going to follow in my footsteps and also lose a child? So I guess God knew ahead of time I would finally do as He wished.

I also felt God was probing me to write more on soul groups, spiritual evolution and reincarnation. A tremendous amount of information had come through to me concerning all of these. So I knew writing about wisdom was going to stretch my mind.

May 20,1999. M.L. was praying with me and suddenly said, "I see a baby coming to give you a rose. The child is placing it in your hand. I think it is Justin. M.L. softly voiced, I'm hearing, +"Tell my Grandma I love her." A few minutes passed and M.L. again remarked, "This is very strange. I was just told that I gave you a wrong message. That's never happened to me before. The child just told me, +'I didn't say she was my Grandmother.'" M.L. remarked with a puzzled voice, "I wonder what that was all about?"

I chilled inside and said, + "Affirmation, I believe I received the rose for finally beginning to write again. It has been over a year since I have written for the Lord. I thought I was finished, but time has proven that wrong. I started writing again yesterday and I have a feeling it's not going to be easy.

***

Heavenly Text

Since I have finished writing the story about Justin I timidly begin to write the following on evolution which I believe is God's will for me to do.

I know the Catholic church does not endorse or teach evolution or reincarnation, but I do believe the messages I have been given are not contrary to the teachings in the Bible. I know that when Christianity began much was removed from the Bible out of fear, because it was not understood. This is being documented as ancient writings (Dead Sea Scrolls, Nag Hammadi Text and others) are being found and translated. Also, I learned in Bible class at the University of Missouri, that church councils and tribunals discouraged many beliefs and made many changes. I know reincarnation was one of the topics discussed and changed at the Fifth Ecumenical Council (533 A.D.). I found in the Catholic Encyclopedia that Origen, a Greek Theologian, who lived from 185-254 A.D., taught that the preexistence of the soul and its reincarnation in future worlds was beyond question. He was condemned at this Council as speaking heresy. (It follows that the Catholic Church has long grappled with this question.)

I know some individuals are interested in this subject of life after death, while others feel disturbed by the thought, as though the question attacks their faith. For me, pondering on the question has given me a deeper faith and a deeper sense of the mystery of life. Whatever one believes, I feel the topic cannot be lightly put aside.

Gandhi, the great Indian philosopher, once said, "It is nature's kindness that we do not remember past births. Life would be a burden if we carried such a tremendous load of memories." Oh, how true. (Although I now believe we carry cellular memory in our body. I believe God in His goodness watches patiently as we unknowingly evolve.)

Heavenly Text

Recently, I read a poll that states the majority of individuals here on earth do believe in a life after death. In the last few decades there have been more talks, more books, more movies, more near-death experiences, more after-life experiences, and more visitations from the spirit world, which I believe have contributed to the growing interest. After a near-death experience people give accounts of being given the choice to stay or return and how their lives are never the same afterwards. Some review past lives.

What used to be a subject for theologians, physicists, and ordinary spectators, has now become a subject of investigation among members of the scientific community. From Plato, Socrates, Jung, and Einstein, to the modern day Edgar Cayce, Dr. Moody, Dr. Kubler-Ross, Deepak Chopra, the question has evolved into, "Is the transition from life to an afterlife a natural phenomena or a Divine Act?"

Since all of creation is of God, by God, and for God, I contend it could be both natural and divine. For me, it is not difficult to think a soul who once lived can return to be a soul in another body. It makes sense to me that since God is pure love, there is no way He would punish or judge anyone by ending their evolving consciousness. He would simply watch as a person's soul evolves into the spiritual being it was created to be. Possibly through soul groups. I envision God witnessing, observing, and allowing us to grow into our full potential--to become one with Him

For me, it makes sense that life on earth is simply fulfilling our destiny of becoming enlightened spiritual beings. I have come to know and believe that the Spirit world is the real world, and earth is but a training ground. We're told in Scriptures that God created the earth for us. We know that God sent Jesus to help us. Jesus showed us the way, saying we could become like Him. He even said we could do greater works than He, (John 14:12) even to the point of being able to move mountains. (Matt 21:21) He also told us we would have to suffer on earth in order to gain eternal life. Jesus showed us that rising from the dead is part of life. He also demonstrated ascension. Are resurrection and ascension also a reality for us? Wasn't I told "Your daughter/son lives?"

Since life is our destiny, and God's plan, why wouldn't we make choices to return, over and over again, to reach our full potential? To say that perfection takes a long, long time would be an understatement. If it took nature ten million years to build the Grand Canyon, why would it just take seventy or eighty years to build a man's soul.

It seems to me we are all here on assignment. Each level of awareness that we reach we gain a clearer picture of the whole. My experiences are no exception. In fact, as I've grown spiritually, my destiny seems to proceed faster, my God messages are clearer, my thoughts have broadened. To me, it appears we all have a mission or a goal to reach, and we are guided to the right place in time. Then free will takes over; we either conform or we don't. We would all proceed much faster if we kept our will in line with God's will at all times. I believe we reach our life's purpose when we work in unison with God's will effortlessly. God messages + abound. This is the path I walk.

Spirit guided me to selected verses in Scripture to add additional thoughts. I've also added my thoughts. We began with Isaiah.

"For my part, this is my covenant with them, says, Yahweh, My Spirit with which I endowed you, and my words that I have put in your mouth, will not disappear from your

Heavenly Text

mouth, nor from the mouths of your children, nor from the mouths of your children's children for ever and ever, says Yahweh." (Isaiah says there will always be prophets who will be speaking His Word. 59:21)

"Bring back my sons from far away, my daughters from the end of the earth, all those who bear my name, whom I have created for my glory, whom I have formed, whom I have made." (Was Isaiah telling us we return? 43:7)

In Ezekiel The Lord Yahweh says, "I am now going to open your graves; I mean to raise you from your graves, my people, and lead you back to the soil of Israel. And you will know that I am Yahweh, when I open your graves and raise you from your graves, my people. And I shall put my Spirit in you, and you will live, and I shall resettle you on your own soil; and you will know that I, Yahweh, have said and done this -- it is the Lord Yahweh who speaks." (Is this statement saying we come back to help, over and over again, when His Spirit is within us? 37:12-14)

"Yahweh created me when his purpose first unfolded, before the oldest of his works. From everlasting I was firmly set, from the beginning, before earth came into being." (Could this mean all (all as One) was created from the beginning of time, unfolding over time? Proverbs 8:22-23)

"Many who are first will be last, and the last first." (Was it possible Jesus was referring to rebirth of all -- all as One? Mark 10:31)

Jesus says, "I tell you solemnly, there are some standing here who will not taste death before they see the Son of Man coming with his kingdom." (Is Jesus telling the disciples that they will be returning over and over to help bring about His Kingdom? Is the Christ within each of us doing exactly that? All of us as One evolving over time, as we find Christ within

Heavenly Text

us. Matt 16:28)

Jesus spoke of rebirth to the apostles saying, "Elijah is to come to see that everything is once more as it should be; however, I tell you that Elijah has come already and they did not recognize him but treated him as they pleased; and the Son of Man will suffer similarly at their hands. The disciples understood then he had been speaking of John the Baptist." (Jesus told us clearly that a soul had indeed returned in another body. Does this apply to all of us because we are all One? Matt 17:12-13)

John wrote in the following scripture, as if those questioning believed in reincarnation. "They asked, 'Are you Elijah?' he said, 'I am not,' 'Well then, they asked 'Are you the Prophet?' He answered, 'No.' So they said, 'Who are you?' 'What have you to say for yourself? So John said, 'I am, as Isaiah prophesied; a voice that cries in the wilderness: Make straight way for the Lord.'" (Was Jesus simply telling us He was part of the One? John 1:19-23)

Solomon wrote in Wisdom, "I had received a good soul as my lot, or rather, being good, I had entered an undefiled body:" (I wonder if Solomon isn't saying he chose to return?)

"In other words, when we were baptized we went into the tomb with Him and joined Him in death by the Father's glory, so we too might live a new life." (I ask, could Paul by saying new life, be speaking of more than one life for a soul? 6:12-14)

Also in Romans, "That is why you must not let sin reign in your mortal bodies or command your obedience to bodily passions, why you must not let any part of your body turn into an unholy weapon fighting on the side of sin; you should, instead, offer yourselves to God, and consider yourselves **dead men brought back to life** (my emphasis); you should make every part of your body into a weapon fighting on the side of

Heavenly Text
God; and then sin will no longer dominate your life, since you are living by grace and not by law." (Romans 6:13)

The previous Bible quotes I used are from the Jerusalem Bible. But I found in Psalms in the Scofield Bible, at the beginning prayer of Moses, "Thou turnest man to destruction (dust); and sayest, Return ye children of men. For a thousand years in thy sight are but as yesterday when it is past, and as a watch in the night. Thou carriest them away as with a flood, they are as asleep; in the morning they are like grass which groweth up. In the morning it flourisheth, and groweth, in the evening it is cut down and withereth." (Psalms 90:3-3)

The Gnostic Gospel, Pistus Sophia, quotes Jesus as saying that, "souls are poured from one into another of different bodies of the world."

I'm sure there are probably many other scripture passages than those that Spirit has guided me to, but these resonated deeply. It is becoming clearer and clearer to me that we are One and that we come from the unknown and go on moving into the unknown. My +'s affirm this for me. And I know Jesus wants me to communicate this to others.

I offer my following evolving thoughts: Our bodies are mortal. Our being, our soul, our consciousness is immortal. Our body gets tired and we die. Then our true being, our soul, our consciousness could continue in the unknown until it decides to return to become more enlightened. Our life's purpose becomes known as we progress in understanding and knowledge. The process could repeat itself over and over. Then once a soul becomes aware of itself, the plan, the purpose for life, the soul could transcend into the knowledge of the unknown. Then rebirth, reincarnation, would not be needed because one would be part of all. Then it would be possible for one to choose to return to aid mankind. I believe this is done in soul groups. (Only God knows for sure.)

My favorite quotes from Jesus that are in the Bible, "I am the resurrection. If anyone believes in me, even though he dies he will live, and whoever believes in me will never die. Do you believe this?" (John 11:25-26) - "As He is so are we." (John 4:17) "I am in my Father and you are in me and I in you." (John 14:20)

I respond in prayer, "Yes, Lord I believe this. I know I am one with You. I wait patiently, daily, for You to continue to show me the way. I believe this generation of Your children are Your descendants. We are the descendants of Abraham. I believe together we can bring about Your heaven here on earth. I don't totally understand all but I do believe all is possible with You. I believe and know in the core of my being that Pam and Justin have found the way. Thanks for Your trust in me to give these messages to the world. Thanks for the deeper wisdom that You continue to convey to me. I marvel at the experience You introduced to me. Thanks be to God. Continue to give me courage. I love You as You love me."

I believe You have been proving to me the ancient wisdom lesson You gave me several years ago, + *"As a child of God, when we let go of our perceptions of reality as we know them and embrace the mystery (mysticism), we can then learn to utilize the energy (Spirit) of the universe, and become one with the Light (God.) Then we win eternal salvation. This is what Jesus taught us by His life and Resurrection. We can then expand the mind further through meditation and master the technique of ascension (bi-location/astral travel), which has been demonstrated by Jesus, Saints, and Yogis. Then the universe opens up and becomes our playground. Death will be*

Heavenly Text
no more. This will be the Kingdom of God."

Dreams of Awakening

Again, there was a lapse of time at the computer but my insides were stirring again. This time I felt the prompting of the Lord to write more about dreams. Dreams, mind you, not visions. I chuckle when I think of : "Old men shall have dreams, young men shall have visions. . . (Joel 3:1) Does this mean I'm now old in age? Or old in wisdom? I hope the latter, since I am not yet even sixty years of age.

As I write this it's the year 2000 and I've had some amazing dreams. I've been very busy this past year in my healing ministry, laying on of hands, doing Spirit/energy work, and teaching others to do the same. Typing had not seemed to fit into my schedule, but the time seems right again to write. It's as if I hear my angels saying, "Where have you been? We have so much to share with you as you share of yourself."

Shakespeare wrote, "We are such stuff as dreams are made of..." I believe this to be true. I believe God has always used dreams as a way of communication. Jesus' life began with angels and dreams. Dreams are mentioned in the Bible over and over, (some seventy times) in both the Old and New Testament. Yahweh said, "Listen now to my words. If any man among you is a prophet I make myself known to him in a vision, I speak to him in a dream. (Numbers 12:6)

The early church regarded dreams the same way they did

Heavenly Text

the Bible--as revelations from God. Dreams come from a source that is quite beyond our conscious control. They seem to abide within us as an unconscious source of wisdom--a kind of superior intelligence. I believe much of the Bible is the story of the breakthrough into the human conscious mind via the unconscious. And this is still happening today. Our dreams are the voice of God experienced in yet another way.

I've always paid keen attention to my dreams and have often written about them. I have small dreams, big dreams, short dreams, long dreams. But the ones I pay the most attention to are my prophetic dreams. Dreams out of the ordinary. Dreams that give meaning and purpose to my life. Dreams where I feel God is speaking to me, prompting me to pay attention. To me, they are nothing more than extended God +'s. I consider my dreams a channel of information for my soul from the Divine.

I believe I have had many prophetic dreams but this past year the pace has picked up. I wonder if my education in dreams followed my education in visions so that I might help others interpret both. I share my time in dreamland hoping you will be encouraged to pay attention to yours. I believe we can learn to view each of our dreams as a scene from a movie - the unconscious.

Before I retire each night, I thank God for the day, ask for God messages in my dreams, and then I explicitly ask for help to remember them. I then always question why a particular dream comes to me. Try it, it works. Discover the closeness of God and join in His fun.

I own the book, *Encyclopedia of Dreams, Symbols and Interpretations*, by Rosemary Gulley. I have used it for years to help me interpret my dreams. After a remembered dream, I immediately write it down. I then often look up the

Heavenly Text

interpretation of symbols, dwell on my feelings and interpretations, and try to make sense of what Spirit is relaying to me. The author recommends, as many dream analyzers do, to see yourself as each of the characters in the dream, to analyze the feelings you experienced during the dream, and pursue deeper meanings from all you can recall. If I keep thinking of a dream for many days I know it is very powerful and meaningful and I continue to search for its many hidden messages for weeks. Sometimes it's months later that I get the full impact of the dream's meaning when I realize the dream has come to fruition. When I type my dreams out in my writings their meaning seems to become even more clear, more enhanced, and more enlightening.

January 16, 2000. A night of two remembered dreams. The first dream I was frantically shopping in a grocery store. I couldn't check out because I couldn't find everything I wanted. I went to another store, then another store, collecting something at each. I finally went back to the original store and checked out everything I had collected from everywhere. The time in the dream seemed confusing but finally I figured out what to do. (Boy, is that true to my life. I search, I search, I read, I read, I process, I process, always looking for the best way and the right way. And it does seem I finally figure it out. Is it time for me to figure things out again?)

In my second dream, I was having trouble buying a ticket to catch a train to get home. Someone sent me downstairs in the train station to see a man who they said would be able to help me. The very kind man pointed to a train that we could see outside of the station and said, "I'll be traveling on that train. You can come with me." I ran up upstairs to get my luggage. When I came back I started to go outside to board the

Heavenly Text

train and the man gently touched my arm and said, *"Just wait here for awhile, the timing has to be just perfect. We need to wait for someone."* He said *"The train will not leave until I give the command. Frantically I replied,* "If we wait the train might leave, I've got to get home." He gently assured me, *"Trust me, and wait here."* +

Upon awakening I whispered, "Thanks God, your special messenger was just reminding me to be patient, that all is in Your hands, trust, and You will take care of all. No need to worry and scurry about. In Your time I will know and understand. I just need to trust in following my destiny. Thanks for the reminder."

January 17, 2000. I had a vision. + I saw three full-bodied spirits. They seemed to be somewhat overlaid but I could distinguish that there were three bodies of light. I saw a door, opened about three quarters of the way, and the spirits were standing to the backside of it. In the front of the door I saw two hands that I knew to be mine. Then suddenly something seemed to bubble up in my hands. I thought stigmata but then decided it looked like two black rocks. I questioned the meaning? Then the vision faded.

("I know God, that although I witness Your miracles often, I know I have much to learn. Were the spirits my guides, my angels, that watch over me? ")

Then that day at Mass, Father Charlie gave a short sermon on the Scripture of the day. The reading was about David and Goliath. Fr. Charlie posed the question, "Was David that strong, or was God in the Rocks?" Bingo! + An answer to my vision. Of course, I thought, God wants me to remember that He is in my hands, nothing to worry about, He will lead me and guide me just like He did David. I approached Fr. Charlie and shared my insight. He said nothing. I know he is still perplexed and doesn't understand.

January 23, 2000. In this inspiring dream, a friend and I were walking on a sidewalk when we came upon a gate. Above the gate was a sign that read, "You are entering a walk through beautiful homes and gardens." Suddenly there were gorgeous colors and flowers everywhere in groomed yards and gardens. As we worked our way through the circular paths we saw a cat. I thought the cat acted strangely. It seemed to be warning us of something. Then we saw a long, shinny, black snake twisting its way along the ground. Shortly, we came upon a lady who was holding a flower pot of greenery that had only one flower blooming on it. She passed her hand over the plant and the entire plant instantly bloomed into white flowers. Then she passed her hand over the flowering blooms and they vanished. I asked if I could try. I passed my hand over the greenery and it instantly bloomed. I was thrilled. + End of dream.

I processed this dream over many days. I remembered the beauty of the dream, the cat symbolizing my feminine side, the snake symbolizing the male, not being afraid of the snake, and using my hands to add beauty. I felt the dream was telling that my masculine and feminine, yin and yang were coming into a greater balance. I knew this complete balance of the body (Kundalini) is what I had been working towards for years -- ever since I had begun Spirit/energy work. Throughout these past few years I had, at times, experienced this amazing vibration. I felt it gently go through my body but I have not been able to sustain it on an ongoing basis. I believe that when I can reach this balance, I will be drawing closer to God and He will be drawing closer to me.

Heavenly Text

February 12, 2000. I awoke with a sudden jolt + and was startled to find myself in my bed. I could hardly breathe. I had been jolted awake from being in China. I remembered in the dream being in the market place, where everyone was wearing kimonos, including myself. I remembered walking along a beautiful body of water. I was trying to find a bridge.

The dream seemed authentic. Had I lived in China in another lifetime? Or did I have the dream because of my love for oriental decor? I remembered dreaming many years ago that I was in China and was speaking Chinese. In that dream I actually knew what everyone was saying although we were all speaking in a tongue that is foreign to me. Regardless, I think this dream is telling me I'm getting ready to cross a bridge. An important bridge in my life. Or possibly my writings will be a bridge for many?

February 16, 2000. I went to Kentucky to spend a few days with my mother. She had congestive heart failure the last week of December. When she was in the hospital they also discovered that she had also previously had a silent heart attack. Her heart is now only working thirty percent. She is 85 years old, tired from raising a large family of nine children, and we know her time to return home to God is getting closer. She is getting more confused and forgetful. I'd been keeping in daily contact with the family trying to decide if and when I should go home. I know she is in good hands because my brother Chris, who is single, lives with her. I had asked God to please open a space in my calendar and show me the appropriate time for me to go home.

I began to notice a window was opening on my calendar when no one called to schedule appointments for the third week of February. A perfect time. I went to Kentucky by

Heavenly Text

myself. I took my massage table hoping to get to use it. To my surprise and delight, mom did agree to let me do Spirit/energy work on her. I also tried to pamper her personal needs in any way I could, manicures, massaging her feet and hands, fixing her hair, etc. Each evening as I shared Spirit/energy and prayed over her I prayed to God that if she was to remain with us, to please give her a decent quality of life.

We talked about her future, her possible death, her past. I asked her if she wanted to come and live with us in Missouri and she thanked me but felt she wanted to stay in Kentucky. She told me she would be happy to go live at the Loretto Motherhouse in Nerinx, Kentucky if she could no longer take care of her personal needs. (The Loretto infirmary is run by the Loretto nuns. It is where the Loretto nuns take care of their retired older nuns, and at times, if rooms are available others. Since my Great Aunt, Sister Sienna, helped to start this infirmary we felt Mom's chances of getting to stay there were good.)

Mother seemed to enjoy the deep relaxation Cranio Therapy brings. In her times of quiet we were able to communicate on a depth that I didn't seem to be able to reach with her during the day. Her feelings that she seldom shares sprang forth and warmed my heart. She shared with me things that she had never shared before. It was good. In the days that followed she began to respond to the energy work of Spirit. I began to see her dress herself, witnessed a more balanced walk, and saw her show a better acceptance of her condition. I heard her comment to different ones on the phone, "I don't know what Nancy does, but it sure does help me."

At last, I witnessed and heard her acknowledgment of what I do. How long have I waited for this? It brought a peace

Heavenly Text

to me. Also, I am at peace with giving her back to God whenever that time arrives. I know she's tired.

I pray, "God, when her time comes I know You will be by her side and will gently take her home. I wonder, is this the bridge I was getting ready to cross? How much of me is an aspect of her?"

February 19, 2000. I had an interesting dream the night I returned home from my visit in Kentucky. I dreamed I was returning home from the hospital after having had a double mastectomy. Erv acted like nothing had happened and was not helping me around the house. He didn't seem to notice or care that I'd had surgery.

Was losing my breast showing me I was losing my connection to my mother? I seemed to have played the mother role, her the child role. I know breast symbolizes nourishment and love. I felt this is what I had experienced in my time with her. Was the dream telling me mothering was over from my mom? Or had she shared something with me we did not understand? I had discovered she had some of the same identical marks on her body that I do. I had found it intriguing that she had a lump on the bottom of her foot in the exact same place where I had my foot surgery.

I spent a great deal of time thinking about all of this on my return drive home, realizing how close we are tied to those who bear us, physically, spiritually, and chronologically (DNA). Descendants from God down a line through eons of time. Our ties are close, our bodies reflect it, our backgrounds reflect it, our lives unfold because of it. I wondered if somehow I was bringing myself, or the lineage of our family, into a physical and spiritual atonement. At one with God in the way He has designed for us all to do. Was I releasing some of the feminine

Heavenly Text

to connect more with my masculine? Was mother going to die soon? I was confused.

February 28, 2000. The following was an incredible dream for me. In my dream I was in Kentucky. My brother Chris was putting up a huge, cedar Christmas tree in mother's living room. He had decorated it with live animals. As I viewed it, I saw an owl at the top which seemed to be looking deeply into my eyes. On a few branches under the owl there were two birds, one blue, one red. A cat was tucked back into the branches in the middle of the tree, a golden dog was perched to one side, and two large white lambs were nestled together at the bottom of the tree. I remarked to Chris, "That is a beautiful tree, but not practical. It will be so messy from the animals' waste." He said, "Don't worry, I took care of that. Watch." Then he proceeded to pull the tree aside with a rope and cleaned the floor underneath. Then he pushed it back into the corner. He promised me he would do that often. End of dream. +

When I woke up I clearly recalled and remembered everything. I can still remember the dream as vividly as the night I had it. It was very compelling and powerful. I'm sure the dream contains many messages that I can think of now and probably dozens more that I will understand at a later date.

How was I going to piece this all together? I asked dozens of questions. The following are but a few of my thoughts. What does Chris have to do with this? Is Chris cleaning the mess up for the family? Does this mean the tree has to do with my family tree or just me? Is this about generational healing? Do the animals on the tree represent my brothers and sisters? Who's who? If the tree represents me, is the dream telling me I've grown and my branches are reaching out? Could the

Heavenly Text

animals possibly represent chakra colors? Is each animal bringing its own story? In scripture the story of the blessing of the two lambs says, "This is to be a perpetual holocaust from generation to generation,...this is where I shall meet you and speak to you." (Exodus 29:42) Are the two lambs representing the masculine and the feminine? Representing Pam and Justin? Is God telling me my tree is full and ready to balance itself? Is moving the tree in and out telling me I've been moving in and out? I know I've been on this journey for some time and it seems to me I come and go with many highs and lows. I was sure the future would keep adding depth and understanding to this powerful dream.

March 5, 2000. I was awakened with a lightening strike. + I immediately started seeing the circle that I often see before experiencing a vision. + I saw an enclosed area with movement going on that I didn't recognize. Then I noticed a small arm that appeared to be reaching out from inside a small tunnel. I seemed to be inside viewing this. It seemed to be a tunnel of a white dough-looking substance. At the end of the tunnel I could see a light shining through. Somehow I felt I was in the tunnel and kept going toward the Light. At one point I seemed to slip into water. It was then that I realized I was experiencing a very real lucid dream. There seemed to be frozen water pipes that burst and water was everywhere. Then, suddenly I was again watching the white substance moving, as if it was breathing. I witnessed the movement of the object, in and out, as I viewed a bright shining Light at the end of tunnel. These experiences lasted for what seemed an hour. I questioned, "Was this Christ Light?" I reveled in the sensations of wholeness, joy, and utter wonderment. I kept asking God, "What is going on?" I only knew that it was a very special

Heavenly Text

mystical experience. I knew I was in the hands of God. But why and what?

I tried to put all of this information together. Was I being shown the womb as a symbol of a new birth? For me? For whom? Was I shown the arm to represent the arm of God? Was I being purified by being submerged in water? Was I undergoing a rebirthing?

I prayed, "I know God that You're guiding me and that this is a very important dream because the experience lasted for such an extended time. Please help me to totally understand. I reveled in Your felt presence."

March 6, 2000. The next day. I had an appointment that affirmed my incredible dream. A female doctor came to my house to experience Spirit/energy therapy. On this day I was thrilled that a physician was interested in experiencing complementary healing energy work. She immediately shared with me that she had just discovered that she was pregnant with her fourth child.

(I want to interject here that last summer Anne came and taught a class on CranioSacral, from *Heart of Listening* by Hugh Milne, D.O. (a book on CranioTherapy that teaches how one can intuitively listen to the energy of the body.) She hadn't been here for two and a half years. Naturally, everyone she had touched in the past was again thrilled to see her, especially me. When she taught the class I learned so much more. Now that I have been taught by many different individuals, I feel even more confident.

Since her classes I've also taught other individuals (from various faiths and denominations) how to sense these subtle energies that are so beneficial in healing work. My services have continued to be more in demand. All who come to me are

Heavenly Text
sent by word of mouth -- angels. My days are full of wonderment and joy as I work for the Lord. I continue to experience many miracles.

I generally mirror in my body what is going on with the person to whom I am attending. Most often I know their needs before they arrive by actually feeling their problem in my body. The disclosure of the doctor's pregnancy at first didn't seem to fit. Especially since I've had a hysterectomy. So, I was questioning and wondering if my dream was telling me something about her baby? Was her baby going to be special? Was her baby being healed?

It was sometime later that I understood and connected this huge +, when I recalled M.L.'s prophecy of April 19, 1999. I reread it and the correlation is so powerful for me. God's timing seems slow to me but it always comes through. It had been nearly a year. It didn't enter my mind at the time of my recent dream that this message was being repeated to me. My dream was showing me that my soul was being healed as predicted in April of 1999. Neither had I put together in my mind that the doctor's pregnancy was an affirmation of the new birth to which I was being introduced. I was symbolically mirroring her pregnancy -- a new birth for me. The similarity of this dream and M.L.'s prophecy was phenomenal to me. + In researching my old writings I also read that on March 29,1999, I had written a message from Jesus that said, + *"Prepare for the clearing of your soul."*

Then I remembered the two-way dream between Anne and me. I looked up that date it was April 16, 1999. That dream had preceded these events. All of the sequence fit together perfectly and now all had been affirmed. I felt I had triple affirmation. I was amazed how my angels guided my mind back and forth to make sense out of what had been relayed.

Heavenly Text

I prayed, "God, I believe You are telling me a new birth is taking place within me. My soul self is coming to life. A closer union with You. This time I did see within and hear within. Thank You, thank You for the affirmations."

March 24, 2000. I had a dream in which I saw and heard the word, Labyrinth. + I knew in the dream that I was supposed to build whatever "it" was that I was seeing. At the time I had no idea what "it" was, I only knew I was supposed to build one. When I got up the next morning, I began my search to find out about Labyrinths.

I found that a Labyrinth is an ancient prayer circle. I learned that in the last few years there had been a Labyrinth renaissance, since the uncovering of a Labyrinth on the floor of a gothic cathedral in Chartres, France. They were being built in great numbers all over the world. A Labyrinth is a sacred path, an ancient spiritual tool, a sacred place that helps us discover the depths of our soul. Walking a Labyrinth is to be a time of reflection, a time to quiet one's self, a time to release anxiety and tension. Walking a Labyrinth helps clear the mind and gives insight to the spiritual journey. (Was my Labyrinth dream also a symbol for me-my soul's journey?)

The Labyrinth was designed by an ancient intelligence that is not fully understood but it is a tool for personal transformation. It reintroduces a walking meditation that was used in an ancient tradition. It gives the everyday person who may not ordinarily go to church or temple a tool for a spiritual experience. It heals and consoles and helps one remember the ancient path where others have gone before. It is a profound devotional tool. Life is a path, a pilgrimage, and walking the Labyrinth makes one take time to find harmony. Labyrinths can be found in almost every religion and every culture. It is a

Heavenly Text
tool for bringing together a community of people regardless of their faith or traditions. It is a place to walk and meditate, to solve problems, to simply talk and pray to one's God.

In my research I found a gentleman, Robert Ferre, in St. Louis who builds Labyrinths. He shared with me the locations of several Labyrinths in St. Louis. I decided the next time I was in St. Louis I would walk one.

March 25, 2000. When my husband, Erv, and I were making love my body began to violently vibrate. This was different then any orgasm I had ever experienced. My body's reactions were extreme. My entire body's vibrations lasted for several minutes. Erv was startled and with a very concerned voice asked, "What is happening to you? Are you having a seizure?" I opened my mouth to say, "It's O.K., I know this is of God," and instead I began to speak in tongues, uncontrollably, for a lengthy time. It was an amazing spiritual encounter. One I will never forget. I knew I had reached a union, a balance, and my body was telling me so. I called it my "Grand Mal" Kundalini. I knew in my heart my dreams of union with God had come to fruition. I was overwhelmed with wonderment and delight.

Books describe this Kundalini power coiled near the base of the spine the serpent power. Over the years, I've had the advantage of capitalizing on the writings and teachings of many astute individuals that have helped me come to understand the importance of this spiritual balancing and awakening.

I have previously read that a serpent has long been a symbol of the creative life force within humans as taught in Eastern traditions. This Kundalini or "serpent fire" lies coiled at the base of the spine. As one grows and develops, this primal energy is released, rising up the spine. This in turn activates energy centers in the body and mind, opening new dimensions and levels of awareness, health, and creativity.

I now believe and know this is what Jesus was talking about when at His Ascension He declared, "..... they will have the gift of tongues; they will be able to handle serpents; they will lay their hands on the sick who will recover." (Mark 16:18)

I'm not big into astrology, but I have friends who are. I know in scripture we are told to watch for signs in the sky and heavens. I've read that astrologers have said that in the first week of May of 2000 our earth would be coming into a grand alignment with all seven planets, the moon, and the sun. They are calling this an astrological phenomena which will affect many. It is being called the window into the new millennium, a time of new birth, an awakening. An awakening of the feminine energy within. That it is no coincidence, that nine months ago we had the total solar eclipse and the grand cross in the sky. The heavens were announcing that in nine months there would be a birth of newness in the world, an elevating and awakening of humanity into a more advanced evolution bringing us back into balance with our souls. A raising of our consciousness. I'd read that these present day astrological signs will go down in history as a turning point for mankind.

It appeared God was using me as an example to write about this alignment. He wanted me to tell mankind. I felt He was using me to teach a wisdom message to the world. A huge +.

As the planets were moving into alignment so was I. Since my "Grand Mal," I have experienced a new kind of orgasm when making love, and a strong Kundalini energy on a regular basis when meditating. I've reached a certain balance

Heavenly Text

in my life that makes me more in union with God. I'm able to reach an intimacy with the Divine that I believe St. Teresa of Avila described in her writings. I believe my soul was awakened and brought into alignment as predicted by my previous dreams.

I understand that each of us has a male and female side, yin and yang, that needs to be in balance. I now know that one has to balance the chakras in their body to bring about this balance. I understand that once we are in balance, in mind, body, and Spirit, we can experience God in a physical way -- in a felt union. "When you make the two one, and when you make the inside like the outside and the above like the below, and when you make the male and female one and the same, so that the male not be male nor the female...then you will enter the kingdom." (Gospel of Thomas)

When we come into total balance, when the soul has reached a purification, and we come to know ourselves, we know that we are in union with the Father and we are his sons and daughters. "Spirits of men are made perfect." (Hebrews 12:23)

I now understand what being a son/daughter means. His message that we can become like Him and do His works is an attainable goal. In fact, I believe it should be our only goal here on earth: learning to become one with Him in order to gain eternal life and help spread His Kingdom here on earth. This union, Kundalini or cosmic orgasm, is a felt presence that is for **All**. (Much later I heard that this is sometimes called karezza.)

This union with God helps explain to me how Mother Mary so loved the Father, that their union brought about Christ. The experience of Jesus on earth was not merely of the Father but also of the Mother - His Mother, our Mother, who represents the Divine motherhood of God, the feminine. I now understand what Jesus meant when he said, "You are the bride, I am the Bridegroom." This feeling of union is a feeling of bliss that could be compared to a physical orgasm yet more blissful and all encompassing. I wonder if this is the Baptism of Fire mentioned in scriptures? Uniting the male and female counterparts within us brings us to a whole and completeness with God. Kundalini raises one's consciousness. I praise and thank God for experiencing His Love and His Wisdom in this way.

I believe this is what John is telling us. "When I am lifted up from the earth, I will draw men to myself." or "Believe in the Light and you will become sons of the Light." Also in James, "Draw near to Him and He will draw near to you." There is no doubt about it. When we come to know God, God makes Himself known to us in a profound way. Some call experiencing this Kundalini energy "enlightenment."

Now that I have felt this power I meditate to reach this awareness. When in a meditative state I breathe deeply and deliberately. I feel God is breathing in me and through me. I say and think the word, "God," as I breathe in. I intentionally pull His Spirit/energy up through my body and visualize it going out the top of my head. As I exhale I feel His breath roll over me like a cascade of water cleansing and refreshing. I feel His breath surround me. I continue this until we become one. My body vibrates with a physical sensation that cleanses and balances. I feel a peace, a calm, a sense of being, a sense of who I am. + "As He is so are we." (1 John 4:17)

I've known for sometime that the word **Spirit** comes from the root word breathe - to live. Spirit is known as God's breath in every religion and spiritual tradition. I know and understand

Heavenly Text
by using His Spirit, our breath, we can come into union with Him. Simply by that relaxing and feeling into the breath, we bridge, the gap between Spirit and matter.

I pray, "Thank you, God, from the depths of my heart for leading me so that I have "at last" been able to reach this union with You on a consistent basis. I know my energy work, my dreams have been preparing me, but I didn't totally understand until NOW. We can only speak to what we know. I now know. I know this process and bliss is available to all, male and female alike. I know it takes time, patience, love, understanding, courage and trust. I know You are constantly calling us to this level of consciousness at this time in history. Thank You for the power I feel. I pray all will discover Your power in this way. For me, Jesus, this is what it means to be created in Your image and likeness. Please help me to sustain this balance in my life so that I can be of better service to You and others. I'm in awe, God, and wondrously looking forward to the adventurous future You have in store for me. Enlighten me daily, help me to enlighten others. Your wonders never cease to amaze me."

I recall years ago my vision of the Phoenix delivering a seed to me. I wrote about this *in Heavenly Text Vol*. I. I now better understand the meaning of that vision. I believe we are all experiencing the chaos of rapid change at the end of a great cosmic cycle. Just like the Phoenix, we are passing through the fire that destroys the old ways of doing things. As the seed is planted, we grow. Through this confusing time the Phoenix reminds us we will be released and ascend into a new life cycle. The seed is the word of God. (Luke 8:11) I have been fortunate to hear the word of God, to heed His word, to continue to grow in His ways. Thanks be to God.

Heavenly Text

April 10, 2000. In my dream I was attending some kind of church ceremony. A man in a white robe, who I thought was a high priest, pulled me aside. He laid hands on my head. While my head was bowed I saw a cross dangling around his neck. He then reached over several people in order to reach another person and laid hands on the head of that individual. It was very obvious that the two of us had been singled out and were receiving a special blessing or anointing. I heard, +*"You two will go forth."* + or was it *"You, too, will go forth?"*

Afterwards, I processed. Why this? Does this add something new? Is there another person? Is it my higher self, my soul, my soul mate? Is this blessing like the blessing of Aaron? Is this vision telling me we can all be anointed into the priesthood of Christ?

In Hebrews, Paul discusses the authentic priesthood of Jesus Christ. I believe Paul was telling us that we are each called by God, as was Aaron, to be a priest. "No one takes this honor on himself, but each is called by God." Paul wrote, "Here we have an anchor for our soul, as sure as it is firm, and reaching right through and beyond the veil, where Jesus has entered before us on our behalf, to become a priest of the order of Melchizedek, and forever. "

I prayed, "Are you telling me, God, that my writings are for all people, that they are not just for ordained priests? Or was it I who thought you meant ordained priests and now you're telling me we are all capable of being priest in God's eyes? Was my dream a spiritual type of ordination? Keep nudging me God, I'll eventually understand all. I'm trying to piece the puzzle together."

April 30, 2000. I had a dream about roots. I was aware that a tree in a huge clay pot needed to be replanted. As I took

Heavenly Text

the tree out of the pot I realized the roots were very, very long. I stretched them out for what seemed a city block. Then I began to roll them up in a ball so that I could get them in another bigger pot. Then I heard, +*"Wouldn't it just be easier to cut them off and start over?"* Then I saw a tree in a huge glass pot with the roots cut off.

My first thoughts were of my recent dream of a Christmas tree decorated with the animals. If the tree and roots represent me, am I again being reminded of the roots of my descendants? Don't old roots sprout again? Am I a descendant from long, long, ago? Does this go back to my last dream of priests and Aaron? Descendants from the sons of Israel? Or is this dream affirming I'm now connected to my feminine and masculine? Or all of the above?

Then when I was talking to a friend about my dream she commented, "Wasn't there a dream in Scripture, in the prophet Daniel, about a tree and roots?" I searched and was dumbfounded when I read that Daniel had interpreted a dream for King Nebuchadnezzar about none other than a tree decorated with animals. Wow! I read the lengthy interpretation of the king's dream. As I read the account, thoughts resonated within me,". . .seven times will pass over you until you have learned that the Most High rules over the kingship of men, and confers it on whom he pleases. . .roots of the tree mean that your kingdom will be kept for you until you come to understand that the heavens rule all. May it please the king to accept my advice. (Daniel 4)

Am I the symbol of the king in the dream? Or do I envision me in the role of Daniel? Haven't I spent years writing and learning to know God in a deeper way? Does it take seven years to reach a union with God? Seven generations? Could the seven represent our seven chakras? I

Heavenly Text

know I've been working on balancing my chakras (I recalled the message of + "the last of your seven sorrows"). Am I being told I've reached an understanding? Am I like Daniel learning to interpret the deep meaning of dreams? Was my last dream the conferring of the kingship of men? Are the roots of old being cut away so I can go forward? I recalled, "And every branch that does bear fruit he prunes to make it bear more." (John 15:2) Am I possibly remembering some of my ancient past? Releasing the past? Powerful, powerful thoughts for me to ponder on.

May 5, 2000. + A vision. I saw a painting of Jesus. It appeared that I was seeing Jesus' entire figure painted on the inside of an arch dome of a huge church. Then I suddenly realized that the arch wasn't a church at all but the roof of my mouth. + Startling! Such a strange visual sensation and knowingness that overcame me.

I prayed, "Are You affirming to me, Jesus, that Your words are in my mouth? I do feel Your breath surrounds me, Your Spirit enriches me, and I know we create together. I love knowing You are within me. I am sure there is probably also more to this symbol. Thanks God, I rejoice, as the vision utterly fills me with joy."

May 13, 2000. Mary's special day. I had two incredibly powerful dreams. In the first dream I met someone new, I believe a female. We went for a long walk on a trail, which seemed to be a tunnel under streets. I had never walked this path before. While walking I suddenly remembered that I had promised to meet someone for lunch and had totally forgotten. It was now 2:45 but I couldn't remember for the life of me who it was I was supposed to meet.

Heavenly Text

Second dream. I was on a train, standing in the front engine with the engineer. I noticed a small tub of water in front of us. A tiny baby was brought in by someone and laid on a blue blanket next to the tub of water. The engineer told me I would be guardian of the baby. He asked me to give the baby a bath in the water. I removed the tiny baby's clothes and submerged it in the water. Then I noticed the baby's tiny eyes opened. They were very blue. The engineer started the train and we went forward. I was looking out the front windows as we moved ahead. +

Immediately, I thought of my earlier dream of January 16, when I was at the train station and the kind gentleman told me, +*"Wait here for awhile, the timing has to be just perfect. We need to wait for someone." The train will not leave until I give the command. Trust me, and wait here."*

So, does this now mean it's time to go forward. Is the tunnel dream reminding me that I get lost at times? Where are you taking me on the train? Is the baby me? Are the blue eyes a reminder of the blue bird? Could these two people I so often see be me and my higher self? Did the child in me die when Justin died? Does the baby represent the child Jesus?

I prayed, "Jesus, I'm beginning to see a pattern here of my past few weeks of dreams. I feel you are telling me that I'm going through a spiritual re-birthing and that you are anointing me and sending me forth with your grace and blessings. I know I work with You. Are You telling me that I have been writing for years and is it now time to go forth? Is it itme? Just lead the way. I'm ready."

Heavenly Text

Going Forward

May 15, 2000. I had an interesting dream before I was to attend a two day conference here in Columbia. I seemed to be in a tower, or attic, and many lightning strikes were coming through the window openings to me. + The dream felt good, even though I was unsure of the happenings.

I asked, "God are you again showering me with graces? Are you preparing me for the next two days? Are you telling me to pay close attention? Will You be speaking to me through this person?"

I was looking forward to the conference the next day to be given by Rev. Robert Keck, PH.D. He is the author of *Sacred Eyes*, a book I read about seven years ago. Back then, I loved reading his book as he helped me connect my thoughts.

When I reached the place where the conference was being held, I spotted and recognized Rev. Keck from his picture in his book. He was standing in the gathering space. I went up to him and introduced myself. Immediately, he said, "Don't I know you? You look so familiar." I replied, "Maybe in your dreams. We've never met but I read your first book years ago and you helped me so much. I'm here to learn more from you and to say thank you for writing *Sacred Eyes*. Your book came at a time when I was wrestling with the connection of Spirit, science, and alternative medicine. Your writings were affirmations for my thoughts." He thanked me and said,

Heavenly Text

"Please call me Bob."

Bob, an ordained Methodist minister, has healed himself from crippling back pain. Many in the medical profession had told him to resign himself to the fact he would be in a wheelchair for the rest of his life. But through meditation, he found the healing power that we all have within us and was able to heal himself. His personal stories, historical knowledge, and deep insights made for an enjoyable two days. He informed us that he had a new book coming out in September, *Sacred Quest,* which is about the evolution of the soul.

Isn't that what I'm writing about? My personal story, of the evolution of my soul. I could hardly wait to read his new book.

I prayed, "Thanks, God for the enjoyable two days and the wisdom Bob imparted to us. I think the dream was alerting me to write about this man, this experience, and to inform me of his upcoming writings. Bob and I have a lot in common. I know we both are writing for You. Thanks for letting me see spirits surround him as he gave his talks."

May 19, 2000. As I was lying in bed waiting for sleep I asked God, "If it's time for our books to be published," I pleaded, "could You please give me a dream, a sign, something to let me know?" Immediately, a vision appeared. + I was thrilled. I saw an open book, with a large hand, fingers spread wide, lying on top of the pages. At the top of the page I read, *"Heavenly Text."* I silently whispered, "What a beautiful title, but it has felt more like a test than a text." I began questioning, "Is this a yes or no? I know this vision is saying the book is in your hands. Or are You saying, "Go forth." I'm somewhat confused. Please give me more information."

Heavenly Text

June 6, 2000. I heard the following in the readings at church. Jesus raised His eyes to heaven and said, "Father the hour has come......I have glorified you on earth and finished the work that You gave me to do. Now, Father, it is time for you to glorify me with that glory I had with You before ever the world was. I have made known your name. Now at last they know that all You have given me comes indeed from You; for I have given them the teaching You have given to me." (John 17 chosen lines 1-8)

I was taken aback. It's how I feel as I share my life in my writings with the world. I know Jesus has taught me, led me, guided me, and encouraged me. I've often been scared, anxious,s and frightened, but thrilled and elated at the same time. I feel I am being pushed forward. I hear, + *"Tell them more. Tell them more."*

Later that day while meditating I heard, +*"Understand My child, each person needs to learn step by step. All are My children. I love all the same. As one grows, one understands. Let Me lead, let others follow. You are for Me, a Light in the darkness of the world. All will become known. Trust, have faith. Others will join to understand as you do. Help Me by being you. I let you be Me in the world. Let Me lead others through you. I'll always be there for you. Be calm. Be patient. We will go forward."*

I prayed, "I know Jesus, that God led the way when You were on earth. I know that now You are leading me. You taught us how to follow His words, how to obey, how to do Your work. I know God is not an object but a way of life. You came to teach us this way of life. God is within each of us. Lead me as I try to follow in Your footsteps."

June 10, 2000. Erv and I made a trip to Kentucky and on

Heavenly Text

our way stopped in St. Louis to walk a Labyrinth. It was made of mulch and rocks. Then later that day we just happened to stop at New Harmony, a tourist town in Indiana. As I got out of the car I was surprised to find we had parked next to a beautiful newly completed Labyrinth. + This Labyrinth was made of granite ($500,000), and is a replica of the Labyrinth from Chartes, France. The people in New Harmony informed us of two other Labyrinths, one in St. Mienards, Ky. and the other in Owensboro, Ky. I knew I was being given a quick education on all of the various types and placements in my path. I began calling it my "Labyrinth Vacation." We walked them all. On our return trip home we stopped in St. Louis again and walked another Labyrinth which was cut in grass.

Returning home from our trip I knew for certain that someday I would build a Labyrinth as I had previously been told to do. But when, how, where, or what kind I wasn't sure. Since I presently was taking donations for charities for my healing work I decided to use the donations for a Labyrinth. I formed a local Labyrinth Association as my new charity and applied for a not-for-profit tax number. All the paperwork went through swiftly and I suddenly was collecting money for a project down the road. I started talking Labyrinth to everyone, trying to locate a place to build one that would be ecumenical and serve the public at large.

July 17, 2000. I had an uplifting dream. I was alone, riding a bike, in the rain down a long path. The dream felt good, peaceful and right. +

This dream confirmed in my heart that I'm following my path as I'm supposed to. My higher self, my soul, is leading the way. I know I often feel I'm traveling this path alone under God's watchful eye. I sometimes feel more connected to the

Heavenly Text

Spirit world than this world. In following my path thus far, I've dealt with the turns and the crossroads as they have come and gone. I know I will experience more surprises and hardships as I'm guided through my journey. I know in the past that my pains and sorrows have brought heart centered compassion and will continue to do so. I thought of the Labyrinth path with its many spirals and turns.

I prayed, "God, I'm ready, I don't care what others think. Lead me down the paths You feel are appropriate. Help me be for You what You are for me."

July 18, 2000. While meditating I heard, +"*This is for you.* + *Write down* **"The Preferences for the New Order."** I saw the words in bold letters like I typed here. "How interesting," I thought to myself, but what should I type. I heard, + *"One: Learn to honor thyself."* I immediately thought of Moses and his receiving the Ten Commandments and receiving the words, 'Honor thy father and mother'. I thought, "How gentle this is. Not commandments but preferences." I heard nothing else. Was it because I started thinking instead of listening? I think so.

I prayed, "Thanks, God, for the reminder and I'll be anxious to hear more of Your preferences when You think I'm ready. Help me Lord to learn of Your presence twenty-four hours a day. Help my scattered thoughts to stay out of the way."

July 25, 2000. I had a vision. + I saw lots of Light. I experienced major Kundalini feelings over and *over. I heard,* + "You need to be in balance. We are changing your vibrations again." I saw a baby being prayed over. ("Thanks God,"" I certainly feel like a baby learning Your ways.")

69

Heavenly Text

July 30, 2000. In the night I heard clearly: +"**Preferences.**" I silently listened.

1. *Learn to honor thyself.*
2. *Learn to be still.*
3. *Learn to listen for guidance.*
4. *Learn to forgive.*
5. *Learn to create.*
6. *Learn to be and to be free.*
7. *Learn to be one with Me.*

I immediately got up and wrote the preferences down before I forgot. I prayed, "Thanks, God. I have heard You explain many of these things in Your messages. I guess I'm not always living what I know. Teach me more. Continue to help me to help myself. Are you going to explain these further to me? Or am I just being told to learn to live them? I patiently wait for Your guidance. I'm trying to follow. It sounds to me that in essence we become the total of the choices we make. I know deep meditation opens me to a blissful state. I find the longer I can hold this state, the deeper the union with You. Since I've learned to go within I've discovered You have been there all along. Thanks, God, for the continued teachings of Your ways."

August 18, 2000. Today I read *The Return of the Bird Tribes by Ken Carey. I* found it especially intriguing because of my repeated encounters with birds. Carey wrote, "The rainbow is a half of a circle to remind us that we must complete the rainbow's circle in our lives, through our lives, through living in harmony with the earth and her creatures, through living in harmony with the laws of nature and through living in

Heavenly Text

peace with other nations around us.... The rainbow is a half circle that we must complete in our hearts."

For me, these words triggered the thought of chakras, which I know are the colors of the rainbow. I have been writing about balancing the chakras to bring about balance in our hearts. God said to Noah, "Here is the sign of the covenant I make between Myself and you and every living creature with you for all generations: I set my bow in the clouds and it shall be a sign of the covenant between Me and the earth." (Genesis 9:12)

I wondered, was God telling us we would complete the rainbow circle by balancing our chakras? Is balancing the chakras completing the circle of life? Is balancing the male and female explained to us in many ways throughout the Bible and we are just now getting it? Maybe our forefathers did not arrive at these interpretations because they did not understand the chakra system of the body. I then got chills + when I read in the Book of Revelation, "I turned around to see who had spoken to me, and when I turned I saw seven golden lamp-stands and surrounded by them a figure, like a son of man." (Rev.1:12) Was John seeing the balanced, enhanced, illuminated chakras of Christ? Was God explaining to us, through John, how our bodies could become balanced and enlightened? Is the Book of Revelation explaining the unveiling and understanding of ourselves?

August 20, 2000. Another new lesson is taking place in my life at this time. I am being introduced to crystals. I've always questioned why some people are so enthralled with quartz crystals but I've never tried to learn anything about them. Then last week a friend showed up with a gift of a gorgeous crystal. The large cluster is about twelve inches long,

Heavenly Text

eight inches across, four or five inches thick, with hundreds of clear and smoky quartz crystals, all forming a large cross. I was stunned at its beauty. She also gave me several smaller quartz crystals and explained, "I went to Arkansas and dug all of these crystals. I have had this unusual one of the cross in my house for several years and I felt it needed to be passed on to you." + I was honored with the gifts, but wondered what I would do with them. I thanked her and placed them on a shelf in the room where I do Spirit/energy work.

Within a couple of days another person who comes to me saw the crystals and remarked, "What beautiful crystals. I have a book on crystals. Would you like to read it? The book is all about healing with crystals." I'd always been a little leery, but not wanting to hurt her feelings I replied, "Sure, I'll look through it."

Within two days, another person noticed the crystals and said, "Oh, I didn't know you have crystals, I've got some books that might be helpful to you. Would you like me to bring them to you?" I was beginning to wonder if God brought the crystals into my life for a reason. "Sure, bring the books over and I'll read them."

I also received other comments such as, "I see you have crystals lying on your shelf. That scares me. My church talks against them." and "I hope you aren't into crystals, I think they are New Age."

"Trust me," I answered, "I'm reading and trying to sort this all out. I think God must want me to learn and write about crystals. I've heard lots of different opinions and mixed messages about crystals in the last few days. I also know that I need to be open and let God explain. I'm sure He will send the information I need."

The need within me to know and explain increased. I

Heavenly Text

became interested in piecing together the ancient and modern myths that trace the superstitions down through centuries that helped explain the fascination individuals have with these beautiful objects. I wondered why nature had created such beautiful stones over eons of time?

I learned that rocks, crystals and stones of all kinds have a molecular structure that is always in movement, in a constant state of change. One can see this with microscopic equipment. I understand that crystals are purified forms of matter, made up of atoms, that have formed over thousands of years in the soil of the earth. I wondered if these minerals of the earth were like the bones of earth. There are thousands of different sizes, shapes, colors, and styles. Mother Nature seems to incubate and give birth to a wide variety of exquisite crystalline forms, just like mankind's many different shapes, sizes, colors and styles. In essence we are all created from energy, the same as the earth. The earth is a reminder to us of the billions of years of existence. All is constantly changing and being purified.

I read several books about the use of crystals and other stones for healing purposes. Priests, medicine man, rulers and shamans have worn and used stones for centuries. I learned that some stones are ground and used in potions and medicines. Gems and stones are now being used in the medical field in the treatment of gallstones, surgical lasers, pace makers, and other life-saving equipment. Crystals also have many uses in modern technology including computers, watches, radios, space shuttles and other technology.

I was reminded in my search that in the Bible, in Exodus, the vestments of Aaron were adorned with jewels and crystals to bring protection, and that the emerald was one of the four stones given by God to Solomon. I read that in India in 400 BC, a Sanskrit document laid down the astrological properties

Heavenly Text

of gems. I read about Indians using crystals for diagnosis and treatment of disease. I read that crystals are used in meditation to develop intuition, how they enhance dreams, and inspire healing practices. I read where churches and royalty throughout the ages used crystals for ceremonial rituals and adornment, as it was felt that gems enhanced God's power. Ancient Romans believed opals bestowed the powers of prophecy. The Greeks associated stones with the unconscious and emotions. I read where Pope Innocent III ordered all bishops to wear sapphire rings in order to resist "inharmonious influences." (So even the Catholic church used jewels in various ways in times past. Interesting, very interesting!)

One book I read was written by a Chinese doctor who wrote how stones are used in Chinese medicine. He explained how crystals have memory. He explained how crystals helped enhance energy because they are the purest forms of nature's energy that has evolved over time. He believes crystals are capable of projecting, receiving, or reflecting light. He explained how they could be used in healing, clearing the aura and balancing the chakras of the body. He explained how they can be powerful tools for spiritual enfoldment and as spiritual gifts they can help open and clear pathways for Spirit to flow through the lower body to awaken the memory of the soul. He explained how they should be cleansed by washing and placing them in the sun.

I amazed myself by following his directions and cleaning my new gifts by laying them out to be refurbished by God's energy giver, our golden sun in the sky. When I went to retrieve them I was utterly shocked at the energy emanating from them. +

I silently prayed, "God, You've certainly got my attention. I can feel the power of the Universe radiating from these

Heavenly Text

beautiful objects. What do You want me to do with them? I know they are of the earth and are from You. I know there are many varying opinions on the use of these creations. I trust You will lead me and guide me. Thanks for the information thus far. The eight books I received as gifts have been very enlightening. Continue to teach me Your ways. I'm Yours. I await Your knowledge from above. Lead me and guide me."

September 25, 2000. An exhilarating day of Spirit but also a day of sadness. My good friend M.L., came for her last visit. She was moving to another state. She will be deeply missed. I felt that God was removing one of my direct phone lines to Him.

As we visited, M.L. and I were showered with gifts and lessons. When we were praying together I asked God why I'm unable, when praying with others, to see Jesus and the symbolic pictures that M.L. continuously sees. Immediately, M.L. replied, "I see you surrounded by purple. Jesus is showing me how he has placed a golden cap over your head, it comes down over your eyes. It's there so that you will see only what he wants you to see for your writings." + She continued, "I'm getting the scripture verse....John 20:29."

Our couple of hours together felt special and blessed. We felt God was showing us that our future would still be one of a special connection although miles apart. We looked for the scripture quote in John. We were thrilled to read. "You believe because you can see me. Happy are those who have not seen and yet believe."

Later, we also turned on my computer to look up something and M.L. exclaimed. "That's what I saw. Just like that." She was viewing the background screen on my computer which is purple with geometric designs. She had never seen it

Heavenly Text

before. She commented, "I think the purple was just an affirmation that you are to write what you are shown. If you got pictures when working on people and wrote about those, the book would be huge. I think God's plan for you is perfect."

Then two days later, I was reading back through notes of days spent with M. L. and found that on December 8, 1998 she had told me, "I see Jesus placing a golden skull cap over your head. You will begin to write again on March 19, 1999." That is when Justin died and I started writing *Gift of Wisdom*. (A repeat message, another reminder, another affirmation. Why can't I remember all that you tell me? Thanks, God. Maybe when I finish these writings I will receive the gift of spiritual sight when working with others.). When I later asked M.L. if she remembered the older message she replied, "No way. My mind can't remember messages for two hours after I'm with someone. Certainly, not two years."

October 26, 2000. I was meditating and I suddenly saw Anne in my mind's eye. She said, "You are now a goddess." I felt a tremendous surge of energy. + I then saw Anne and me flying in a huge temple over a large crowd. I immediately opened my eyes and realized I was alone in my bedroom. Yet, the moment had all seemed so real.

Then one day later in mediation, I heard, *"The Goddess is about bringing Divine Love into manifestation."* + I felt God was telling me that He expands through each of us.

Another day I read an article on the internet that stated: "Integrating the Goddess means we need to love and nurture our bodies in order to develop a higher consciousness. When we integrate the Goddess we are bringing back the power of the Heart and the Power of Love into every part of our life. Integrating the Goddess means learning to see, hear, and speak

Heavenly Text
from the heart. This will develop more wisdom so that we can embody a conscious ascension and a conscious enlightenment."

November 6, 2000. I saw a long list of names and dates in a vision ending with the date November 20. I did not see the year. I witnessed the list being cut off at that date. + I just knew in my heart that it meant things were going to be different after that time. I wondered if it was this year, the past or the future. (I recalled that it was on November 20, 1998, that I had a profound note from M.L., which stated I was going to write a book for priests. Also on November 20, 1997, I had experienced a vision of seeing written material on red paper.)

November 26, 2000. I had a wonderful dream of a beautiful white horse coming to visit me. I went to the door and there was a beautiful white horse. I invited it in. Realizing how gentle and loving it was, I kept petting its nose. Eventually I sat down on the couch and the horse laid its head in my lap. It seemed very normal for this to happen. It was a very peaceful, good-feeling dream.

Then that dream was followed by another dream of me riding up a hill in a car. As I reached the top of the hill I saw a huge wide tornado. There was no escape, no way to avoid it, the tornado was going to get us. I don't remember who the driver was. I woke up.

I've had tornado dreams before and they always seem to be a sign of change. Had something happened on this November 20th to change things?

The next day when I went to church, the readings were from the Book of Revelation, and a white horse. + I asked Father Charlie what the symbol for the white horse meant. (I didn't share my dream.) The following day he brought me a

Heavenly Text

copied page from a book (?) that listed insights into the spiritual meanings of this scripture.

I was intrigued as I read the following lines from the more expanded article: "In the Book of Revelation, the white horse is mentioned in the opening of the four seals. White...the symbol of victory, as is also the crown received by the rider. . .he that sat on him. . .Since Irenaeus, he has often been identified with Christ, who appears sitting upon a white charger. This rider stands for a conquering power whom none can resist. . .usually referring to the coming of Christ."

Then in the *Animal Speak* book, it says "a horse brings with it new journeys. It will teach you how to ride into new directions to awaken and discover your own freedom and power."

I silently asked God, "Are You affirming my awakening? Am I going to get to see Jesus again soon? Am I to die to self more in order to learn to grow in Your knowledge? I do believe you are letting me know I'm doing what is expected of me. I do feel You are constantly imparting more wisdom to me. Thanks."

December 8, 2000. I was with Mark on this day, a fellow Spirit/energy worker. He was having knee problems. He is one of my friends who now sees and receives messages like M. L. (God is good and continues to guide me through others.) Mark commented, "I'm supposed to tell you that you are going to feel the presence of God in a special way today." + "Really," I replied, "I wonder what that will be? I've had many interesting occurrences over the years on the date of December 8." No other messages came through while we were together, so I pushed the thought aside. We did experience some deep healing taking place on his knee during the time we spent

Heavenly Text

together.

That night, during sleep, I was awakened by an audible voice. + This happened to me before while experiencing a vision and I was told by an audible voice to *"Write."* I was awakened this time with a voice saying, +*"Are you sure you want this?"* + I sat up and opened my eyes hoping to see someone. I felt a strong sense and presence of love energy. I answered, *"Yes, I'm sure."* Then I heard, +*"Be sure, after this you can never turn back."*

I looked about with my eyes open and saw nothing. I laid back down. I wondered what I had agreed to. I knew I'd do whatever was asked of me. For days I couldn't get the voice out of my head and wondered over and over to what I'd answered "Yes." I thought often of Mary and how she had said, "Yes." For her it was the birth of a savior, for me I believe it will be the birth of a new me.

Then on December 12, 2000: On the internet I read an article of a channeled message from Jesus to another individual. I was thrilled when I read, "December 8th is the dawning of the new era. There will be no turning back. Some will even hear a voice declaring this new time." +

I prayed, "Alleluia! Thanks God, for the repeated information and affirmation on the voice I heard.

Then in mediation I heard, *"The goal of creation of mankind is to bring Light into matter (our bodies) and quicken it with Spirit, which transforms the physical body into higher vibrations.* +

I know creation is happening at a rapid pace at this time in history. Human beings are being changed. Our bodies are being changed, our minds are being activated. We are becoming different vibrational beings. We are being

Heavenly Text

transformed. Many are going through the transfiguration. We are becoming bodies of Light. I know my body has changed drastically. The changes I experience have been enhanced by the healing ministry that I am part of. I know my soul is evolving.

I know we are becoming multi-dimensional beings of Light. I know that the time is near for Spirit to contact the masses, to bring about the energy of Christ on earth in full force. This is what the awakening is all about.

The story of the expansion of life is coming to many through different awareness; in meditations, in dreams, in channelings, or through visitations from the Spirit world. We need to remember that we are all characters in this story that is unfolding around us. We always have been guided but the pace has picked up. The changes at this time are happening more rapidly and are going to be wondrous.

I've read more than once on the internet that scientists are proving that the magnetics of the earth are changing. Frequencies are rising, and magnetics are dropping. As mankind's consciousness expands and our bodies adapt to the new vibrations and magnetics we can expect many unusual occurrences. I am aware that our universe is vast, that the earth is but a small part of the whole. I've read about the dimensions of the universe, about the hierarchies of the spiritual world, about the vast cosmos that exists.

Lately, it's been intriguing to read many messages on the internet that are channeled from the heavens to numerous individuals. The major networking going on from the various dimensions, councils, and spirit world is mind boggling. I believe many people do not even have a clue that this takes place.

We are all connected. God is the vine, we are the

Heavenly Text

branches. We are all one. So the shifts that are happening to the earth are also happening to all of us. Or is it the other way around. Is the earth changing to our changing? The natural disasters, floods, volcanic eruptions, earth quakes, occurrences of violence are nothing more than the realignment of the earth to help bring about a balance. There is never a reason to fear change. We are now witnessing and living through an interesting time in creation.

December 21, 2000. I had a vision visit of lots of geometric sizes and shapes. I saw cubes, triangles, squares, pyramids, all floating in space. +

I wasn't sure what was being relayed to me. I've read that sacred geometry is the language of light - a mirror of the heavens. Maybe I'm being educated on a level I don't yet understand. I'm sure my intuitive self, my spiritual self, my consciousness absorbed whatever it was supposed to. I remind myself often that I don't always understand the communications clearly from Spirit, but in time all does become clear.

December 24, 2000. I had just settled into my bathtub in the early morning and had closed my eyes, when all of a sudden I saw a sparkling gold light in the distance. + As it drew closer and bigger, I noticed the sparkling light had a cross in the center. I watched this travel back and forth in my mind's eye until it turned into another bright light that took on the shape of a star (Star of David came to mind). Then this lighted star landed on the top of a pointed object. This object began to rise from the bottom of my inner eye's observation and became larger and I realized the object was a pyramid. This picture eventually turned into a circle of green light. (I kept giving

81

Heavenly Text

thanks for the experience, not totally sure of what was happening.) A large circle then came into view. It was surrounded by an outer circle. (An astrology circle-chart came to mind.) Shortly, an arrow began to emerge from the center and traveled to the top left part of the circle, (It would have been about 11 o'clock on a clock). Above this I began to see an outstretched hand pointing to an open book. A white dove was suspended above the book, turning the pages with its beak. It was spellbinding to watch. I was questioning if this was the book I was writing. Then I saw what seemed like the outline of an angel in a circle. This changed into another angel or being of light, then another, and another. Each looking different with different types of wings, different movements, different colors. I kept saying, "Let me see clearer. I need Spirit glasses. The detail is not clear enough. I heard. +"*The pictures will become clearer. You will see this often.*"

This spiritual video lasted nearly thirty minutes. I know for certain the time because my timer for the jetted tub went off, which had been set for thirty minutes. I was in awe and bliss. I still am as I type this.

Afterwards I ran into the family room to share with Erv. My hands were shaking, my face was aglow with energy, as I enthusiastically relayed my meditative experience. Erv remarked, "Your face is so red. Have you looked in the mirror?" I replied, "Yes, I think it's just from the excessive amount of energy." I didn't even take time to turn on my computer. I fetched my pen and began to write so I wouldn't forget. I also drew a picture of the hand, book, and dove as it had been relayed to me.

I'm confident that the message will become clearer as time goes by. I've already had many thoughts. I know that the book of life is in God's hands, guided by Spirit. Was I being assured

Heavenly Text

that what I write is from Spirit? Were the various beings of light teachers? Spirit guides? Is Spirit preparing me for a new form of communication? Was the circle an astrological calendar telling me I've almost completed my circle of life? I know the triangle, the pyramid shape, can have many different meanings. I've always known that the triangle is the symbol for God in many religious denominations. Christian Theology teaches that the Trinity is God the Father, God the Son, and God the Holy Spirit - Three persons in one God. God the Father is our Creator. God the Son is Jesus showing us the way. The Holy Spirit is the wisdom of God in action, or Mankind.

I know a new thought always makes me think deeper, a vision makes me delve even deeper, and this video vision was affecting my whole being. I began to look for answers and information to help me better understand. In my search I found that Jung said visions are encountered by a wider part of ourselves. This wider self can appear as many different symbols. The most common is the circle, representing wholeness, and the cross representing the conscious awareness of that wholeness. Jung suggested that the cross points to the Christ Consciousness as the ultimate symbol of the higher self. He suggested it represents the conscious integration of a physical and a spiritual life into one being--the self realization of the divinity of God that lives within us. His comments resonated. ("Thanks, God. I'm humbled.")

December 29, 2000. Donna, the daughter of a friend of mine, was in town for the holidays. She asked if I had any time available to get together. I've previously shared Spirit/energy work with her. She arrived about ten in the morning. We talked for an hour or so before we began. Afterwards she laid

Heavenly Text

hands on my head. After a brief time she remarked, "Something strange is beginning to happen to me. As I get out of the way and let God use me, my hands are automatically being guided." She was crying and sharing what was happening. "My hands are being pushed away from your head and it feels like an unfolding, an unfolding of petals or something. My hands are making the shape of an inverted cone. Oh my, now, I'm seeing the face of Jesus and it's all in red. Now I'm seeing a bright red heart. A real heart, ventricles and all. It's so red. I'm hearing, +'This is a special blessing'." We were both crying at this point. It was the first time she said she had ever seen the face of Jesus or had received a message so clear. We both were very moved. She felt the message was for me. I told her I felt the message was for both of us because I was praying that God would open Donna's heart to His healing power. Needless to say it was a very moving experience.

When we discussed her vision of the heart, I kept hearing within, +"*God speaks to us in our heart.*" I remembered the marvelous vision of the Exposed Heart of Christ I saw several years ago on Christmas day. I told Donna, "I know our hearts contain the Holy Spirit. God dwells within us. It is in the Heart that we learn to hear the voice of God. I feel the symbol of the heart on this day is the Holy of Holies carrying the presence of God to us. It is through the heart that we reach peace and become one with God. It is in mediation that we connect with the Divine through our heart."

Donna and I continued to talk for some time and were in shock when we discovered it was 3pm. Our time together had flown by and we had lost all track of time. I had shared my experience of the video vision. She said that the light I saw on top of the pyramid made her think of the symbol of the

Heavenly Text

pyramid on a dollar bill. We looked, and sure enough it was very similar to what I had seen. She also asked if the star was a tetrahedron shape, which is two triangles, one inverted over the other. I told her it wasn't crystal clear; I had seen points and thought Star of David at the time. I guess I need to look for more information on both of her thoughts to see if anything resonates.

December 31, 2000. I closed the year by reading Robert Keck's new book, *Sacred Quest*. I highly recommend his book, which is truly a gift. Keck is a bright, gifted, intelligent man. He is a man of integrity who does a wonderful job of historically explaining the evolution of our souls. I believe Keck's following quote explains why I write. "The sacred quest is an attempt to quest after some understanding of the human spiritual journey. How to live a spiritually responsive life and to question where humanity and our lives, our religions, and our spiritualities are going in the future as the twenty-first-century Soul grows within us."

As I write my private story, he writes the history. For me, it is so refreshing and uplifting, to have a comrade in writing. He is someone from the pulpit trying to bring the message to Christians of the world. I'm in good company. ("God, please send more.")

Little attention is paid to the fact a new era is upon us by those in the main stream of life, but I know it is real. It's a pity that the churches and religions of the world aren't guiding their people through these times. God is calling for change and growth, and the ones who could be helping the most seem to be in denial. I know in my heart that this transformation will happen, with or without the blessings of Christianity.

I certainly have not heard anything from the pulpit where I

Heavenly Text

attend church about the evolution of our souls, or even a hint that something different is transpiring in the world around us. I definitely feel a gap. The masses need to hear the messages of change from their spiritual leaders. I believe then people would listen and pay attention.

It seems to me that all religions try to convey what is important, but their practices, rituals, concepts, ideas, and traditions have all gotten scrambled over the years. The negativity that has crept into religions of the world needs to be dropped -- and quickly, so mankind can evolve into the individuals we were created to be.

Thanks to the internet, there is more help circulating among the air waves, but not circulating among the elderly, the non-computer users, the non-conformist, the non-educated, non-believers, or non-interested.

I pray, " God we need help. We need You to help pull all of this information together in a unified way for all religions, cultures, and spiritual searchers throughout our earth to help us unite.

It's a wonderful feeling to know that I'm a small part that has tapped into the bigger picture of life that is unfolding in the heavens. I believe the story of what is happening in the solar system, in the galaxy, in the universe that is creating change on our earth will be a story that is told in a future book. Maybe some of my writings will be in that book. In days of old, we had prophets telling us of the future, and now it seems history is only repeating itself.

Thanks, God, once again for the affirmation, for the added confirmation that I'm not alone in my spiritual thoughts and writings. Continue to accelerate my growth as an evolved spiritual being. Thanks for all of the recent answers to so

Heavenly Text

many of my wonderings and questions. Thanks for being by my side and enlightening me day by day. As I type on this last day of the year, I await with joyous anticipation for the unfolding of the New Year of 2001."

The Century of Change

I believe this decade (2000-2010) will go down in history as a time of tremendous change, opportunity, and enlightenment. A time unprecedented in the history of the earth. A glorious time to be on the earth to witness the unfolding of God's creation like never before. A massive time of transformation. January started out with another interesting experience.

January 4, 2001. Dottie, my good friend and fellow Spirit/energy worker, was at my home. We were exchanging sessions. When her hands were on my head, she suddenly exclaimed, "I see a head of someone, oh my, it's Jesus, and it's all red." + (How wonderful I thought, another person seeing the same thing that I had experienced just a week ago. Dottie had just recently begun to have spiritual sight.) I shared with her my time with Donna. We marveled at the sameness.

We questioned, why red? Questions filled my mind. Isn't red a symbol for blood or fire, a very powerful energy? Isn't red often thought of as the color of suffering and martyrdom for the faith? The supreme sacrifice was made by Christ, so wouldn't it make sense Jesus would be surrounded in red? Is this what Christ consciousness is all about? I remembered several years ago having had a vision in red.

I never cease to be amazed at the privilege of receiving

Heavenly Text
information from a higher source through the doorway that is open in the top of my head or the channel of my heart. It's in those soft places that Spirit speaks and that's why I love Spirit/energy work so much.

My aim has always been to come into harmony with the consciousness of our creator as I have learned to bring in God's power and energy from higher sources. I believe all of God's vessels are part of an inner communication network receiving light and information from other dimensions. A vessel learns how to use that light when he/she uses themselves as part of a divine communication system. We become like spiritual antennas. I believe we help each other unlock information from the heavens.

January 12, 2001. I had a dream of riding in a car. There was a man waving his arms in the middle of the street trying to stop me. I remember feeling some fear, then I passed by without interference. I think I was being told there would be interference but all would work out.

This week I read the book *Infinite Mind* by Valerie Hunt. An enjoyable, informative book written by a scientist, who is now in her eighties. She herself is a healer and explains how she spent her life trying to prove how Spirit/energy works. The book has many graphs and other scientific material to explain the unexplainable. She learned how to measure the human energy field and has confirmed that a person's state of mind affects their vibrational speed of frequency. I would feel comfortable sharing her book with anyone who asked me, "What do you do?" I believe her writings are a + for the world, especially the doubting scientific and medical community.

She explains how our Western world accepts machines'

abilities, but seems to deny the power and control from within the human; how society accepts the fact that surgeons achieve miracles with scalpels, but seem to deny miracles achieved by human beings channeling healing energy; how society accepts x-rays, but seem to deny human vision that can pierce beneath the skin; how society accepts the telegraph, but seems to deny word beyond the human ear, the word from Spirit.

I ask, "Haven't individuals, such as St. Paul and Gandhi, shamans and healers, used mystical consciousness to tap into this universal information?" If we realize their gift can be our gift, we also can learn to tap into the Divine. When we acknowledge mystical wisdom and spiritual power, trust in God, and let Him lead us the doors open to unbelievable occurrences--we rediscover our soul. Jesus used this energy transference to heal, then to resurrect and ascend.

January 21, 2001. A vision. + I saw two books. One very large and a smaller one laying beside it. A hand reached and turned the smaller book over so I could read the title on the side of the jacket. I saw the writing "*Afterwards.*" + The background of the vision was a deep red. I wondered if this was telling me to write a new book or a condensed version of my old writings? Or was I now writing that book? Or another later?

Was I given a message in red three times in the last two weeks, to affirm my writings and communications from the heavens? Confirming the continuation of my soul's evolution? Informing me of the opening of my eighth chakra? I just know I'm not alone in my spiritual awakening, only a part of the massive network being guided from above.

I pray, "Thanks, God, for bringing together information

Heavenly Text

for me to share with people of the world who are searching for your knowledge. As confusing and hard as it has been over the years, I know that I have been fulfilling my destiny. I anxiously look forward to the further evolution of my soul. Thanks for the affirmations. I utter to You the words of other prophets before me, I know that I Am what I Am for Your honor and glory."

When I went to church the first weekend in February, the readings for the Mass were about the prophets giving of themselves and submitting to God's will by saying, "I Am." I had chills when I heard in the reading Isaiah responding, "Here I Am." Then Father Charlie gave a sermon on the significance of the words I AM that I AM. + Coincidence? I think not. This isn't the first time God has lined everything up in a sequence for me in order for Him to get His points across.

I later read in a Catholic periodical an explanation of the Biblical words I AM. It stated that in Hebrew I AM consists of four letters YHWH and when we add the vowels to it, as when we say Yahweh, we begin to interpret its meaning. The root of YHWH is a form of the verb to be and can have three meanings: I cause to be all that exists; I cause to be all that happens; I am always with you. (Reminds me of the Preferences I heard.)

Still later I read *Teachings of The Masters of the Far East* written by Baird Spalding, and he states that man is not his experience, but what he is. He explains: An individual is always that which I AM In Spirit." The "I" in an individual is his identity. The "AM" brings forth whatever an individual embraces. The "I" is the masculine principle; the "AM" is the feminine principle. The "AM" must become immaculate in its embracing power if one is to bring forth that which is in Spirit.

Heavenly Text

"I" which is one's identity in Spirit, and "AM" which embraces all that is in God is the true use of these words. "I AM" that I AM is the embodiment of God. One can never be anything but that which is in Spirit.

I am beginning to resonate more and more with the words of Plato, "But perhaps there is a pattern set up in the heavens for one who desires to see it, and having seen it, to find one in himself." I decided that I now wanted to learn and understand more about sacred geometry. I went to the internet, and sure enough, there was a lot of information. I read for several days. So can you, but the following will summarize what my research pulled from various sources said to me..

The study of ancient writings reveal that art, science, and religions were interwoven and interconnected, especially in the Egyptian mystery schools. At that time, initiates learned sacred geometry as a path to spiritual awakening. Pythagoras (born 580 BC) was first to demonstrate and teach that cosmic harmony was found in the eternal perfection of numbers, the very mystery of life itself. He also discovered that musical notes limited by mathematical relationships, or numbers, produced harmony. He was the first to teach that sound was part of creation. We know that the Bible states, "In the beginning was the Word." Thus, if not for Pythagoras, Christians might not have thought of Christ as the Word. It is known that sacred geometry is the root of all languages.

All the geometric symbols and equations that we are familiar with today originated from ancient times. I read about the Platonic solids, five unique shapes (cube, sphere, triangle, octagon, pentagon), which are crucial to studying sacred geometry (or even regular geometry, for that matter). I read how the progression of life forms through the shapes of these

Heavenly Text

Platonic solids to create life. As humans we start out as an ovum, an atom, that contains the triangle. We move into a tetrahedron shape at four cells, then on to two interlocked tetrahedrons at eight cells, and on. I discovered that it is scientifically proven that the pyramid shape exists in every cell of our body, including our blood. Thus geometric symbols are the basis that lead us into and out of physical existence.

There are many ancient symbols that teach us that there is an on-going repetition of geometric forms no only in human life, but also in nature and the universe. In nature, for instance, the snowflake, crystals, cells in honeycomb, and a cube of salt are but a few. The earth is a sphere, and the entire universe is a geometric design. In other words, sacred geometry is the form that points to Divine order in our reality. We can follow that order from invisible atoms in the body to the stars in the sky.

I read that some believe the most significant sacred geometric symbol is the "Flower of Life," which is a geometric template that contains the blueprint from all geometric forms. This is believed by many to be the blueprint for consciousness. The "Flower of Life" symbol was known to be among the most sacred symbols in ancient times. It contains all of the possible configurations of geometry possible, thus the symbol of the unity of all consciousness and life within the universe. The diagrams explaining all of this are fascinating. I also recently heard that the "Flower of Life" symbol has been uncovered on the floor of the St. Francis of Assisi Cathedral in Italy.

I learned that many believe that sacred geometry is a direct teaching on our cellular level, heard by our DNA, that is causing the human race to change and grow into a higher level of consciousness. I recalled my God message from December:
+*"The goal of creation of mankind is to bring light into matter (our bodies) and quicken it with Spirit, which transforms the*

Heavenly Text
physical body into higher vibrations. +

God is good. He brings me affirmation of His messages over and over. I believe I now understand how light is information of a different nature. I believe Light is the primary frequency of the Infinite Mind. Light brings transformation so we can evolve. I believe Light is Love. I believe we are becoming beings of Light, fulfilling the scripture, "Believe in the Light and you will become sons of Light." (John 12:36) I know I am using God's power and Light in my healing work. More and more I feel this explosion of power throughout my entire body. I know massive amounts of light and love are pouring into me. I know I continue to get stronger and stronger in the ways of the Lord. I also believe this is what Paul is telling us when he writes, "For us, our homeland is in heaven, and from heaven comes the Savior we are waiting for, the Lord Jesus Christ, and he will transfigure these wretched bodies of ours into copies of his glorious body. He will do that by the same power with which he can subdue the whole universe." (Phil 3:20-21)

I began to look back through my visions to discover the different times I had seen geometric patterns. Although I did not understand them at the time, I know they came to me at major times of change in my life. Presuming that is the case, my recent geometric vision and vision video is none other than Spirit's way of informing me that I am once again taking a step forward with God. The pyramid (a triangle) is none other than the symbol for the language of Light. I believe my soul has always understood these communications on an unconscious level.

February 15, 2001. Our daughter Deanna, had a healthy baby girl. They named her Madison. It's been two years since

Heavenly Text

Deanna lost her son, Justin. The doctors had told Deanna the probability of her having another child was slim to none. Then God took over. He surprised them with a new angel.

Deanna again had a difficult pregnancy. She was nauseated for nearly nine months. The doctor induced labor which turned into a long rough day. I didn't know until the next day that there had been some difficulty with the per-cervical. Evidently, it was administered wrong and Deanna got very sick and then partially paralyzed. When she called the morning of the 16th she told me that the doctor was concerned and had kept her in the delivery room for five hours after Madison's birth. About 3:30am, she began to recover.

We had gotten the call from Jeff, on the 15th at about 11pm that Madison had been born and I went to bed. I was having a difficult time sleeping because my legs were cramping and aching. Since I had a bad cold, I was thinking I must be getting the flu. I ached. I got up at 3am and took a bath. When I bathe, I always ask Spirit to cleanse my entire body of all toxins, all disease, all aches and pains, and sure enough, I felt fine after this bath. Then in the morning when I heard about Deanna's ordeal, I couldn't help but wonder, because of the coincidence of the time, if I had also been clearing for her. I had prayed for her throughout the day, and at times, had actually felt labor pains. I remembered how I had previously felt pain in connection with Justin. More affirmation that we are all one, so powerfully connected. It appears to me that unsuspecting, we can integrate into the lives of the ones we love - and the lives of others - on a level of love that is not apparent in our physical reality.

I prayed, "Thanks, God, for your gift of the new healthy grandchild and protecting Deanna's health yet once again. Thanks for continuing to clarify the world of non-reality."

Heavenly Text

March 6, 2001. I kept hearing the word + "conceptual," over and over in my head during the night. I couldn't stop it. I must have repeated the word *"conceptual"* hundreds of times. I kept asking Spirit, "What are you trying to tell me?" I wasn't sure. I'd doze off and when I would awaken, I'd hear again, +*"conceptual, conceptual, conceptual..."*

Then I had a dream. I saw a baby, lying on a pillow. Was this our new grandchild Madison? Was I the baby? Someone was sitting on the bed beside the infant. Was that me? Suddenly the baby opened its eyes, and said, "What am I seeing?" I was astonished that such a small infant was speaking in sentences. The person sitting said to the infant, "That is a rack of clothes. Don't worry, you will remember what everything is soon." (I could also see a rack of clothes hanging by the side of the bed.)

I woke up saying, over and over, the word "conceptual." I got up and looked up the word in a dictionary. "Concept: a idea, a thought, adj. conceptual. Conception: a beginning, the power to form ideas, or concepts."

Was I the baby or Madison the baby? Am I ready for a new beginning? A change of clothing could indicate a change of direction, a new phase of life. Was I being asked to be who I was meant to be? Who was Madison going to be?

While typing the above information, I heard, +*"You are transpiring in the concepts of God's ways."*

I looked up transpiring: "to become known, to come to light."

("Thanks, God, I'm sure in time I will understand.")

March 13, 2001. I attended a meeting at the nursing home for my friend Bill, the quadriplegic. I visit him weekly, but this day we attended a meeting with half a dozen individuals to

Heavenly Text

discuss his needs. I was upset because recently, twice when I had arrived to visit him, his sweat pants were wet, and under his wheelchair was a puddle of urine. I know there are accidents, but twice was upsetting to me, and I wanted to complain on his behalf.

While we were discussing their care and his needs, we all suddenly started smelling the sweetest smell. The window was slightly open and I said, "Are there Hyacinth flowers or roses planted out there? They must be starting to bloom, that odor is heavenly." Everyone agreed. They also smelled the heavenly scent. One lady said, "There are none out there." The sweet smell was so powerful, that she even went to the window to look out and check, and remarked, "I don't get it. Where could that be coming from?"

As I pushed Bill in his wheelchair back to his room it suddenly dawned on me that it was the 13th (Mary's Day). I suddenly knew in my heart that the powerful and beautiful scent had been Mother Mary. + She was there with us, in spirit, letting me know she approved of me speaking up for better patient care at the nursing home. ("Thanks, God. Thanks, Mary.")

March 24, 2001. I attended a workshop put on by Robert Ferre on how to build Labyrinths. I found it fascinating that the workshop was scheduled exactly one year to the date since my Labyrinth dream which was March 24, 2000.

The morning of the workshop I had a vision before I got out of bed. + I saw lots of circles, triangles, pyramids, etc. I immediately thought "sacred geometry" and wondered what was being conveyed to me. I soon discovered at the workshop that the layout of a Labyrinth is a major part of sacred geometry, which Robert spent half a day talking about.

Heavenly Text

I'll share some of what Robert told us. He explained how ancient geometry was originally a division of philosophy; how the philosophers of old discovered geometry by seeking for the truth. By searching for the laws of the universe, they discovered the unchangeable truths of the universe - that circles, squares, and triangles are the laws, the building blocks of creation - what God used to create us. He explained how Roman numerals had no zero, and when the alphabet was created, the zero was added. Then geometry changed and algebra began. Centuries ago, there was a constant tension between scientific progress and religious doctrine in the Arab world, just as centuries later it would be the case in the Christian world. Robert questioned whether changing the alphabet by man was messing with God's creation. He pointed out that it says in Wisdom, "You have ordered everything according to measure, number, and weight." (Wisdom 11:12)

Robert explained how every culture down through the ages used the angles of ancient geometry in building pyramids, temples, cathedrals, and the like because they wanted to create as God created. The Chartres Cathedral in France was built from 1194 to 1220, by the most renowned architect and masons of the Order of the Knights of the Templar. It is a Gothic monument of perfect balance and harmony. It was built to carry on their beliefs and restore the feminine principle to the medieval world. It is believed the builders had access to esoteric wisdom of the classical world. Their knowledge of mathematics and engineering gave birth to Gothic style, which spread across Europe. Its structure is perfect sacred geometry throughout, including a Labyrinth on the floor. The masons built a reflection of their faith. They wanted to teach how walking through the cathedral is like walking through life, from the entrance to the altar, representing the journey of this world

Heavenly Text

to the next. The design was impeccable. Even to the design of the window, a rose, a representation of Mother Mary, the rose of creation and life itself. The image of Mary occurs over one hundred times in the cathedral. (I was intrigued with the connection). It was shortly after the building of this cathedral that geometry changed. The Labyrinth is one of the true ancient geometric symbols passed down from ancient times.

During the workshop, we walked several Labyrinths and built two temporary ones. When we walked the Labyrinth, Robert advised us to ask questions of Spirit and to be open for information. He explained that the Labyrinth influences the natural rhythms of the body and was a method to activate a conversation from our hearts to the Heart of God. During my walk I naturally asked, "Where do you want to be built in Columbia? I'm not having much luck finding a place." I didn't receive an answer, but I knew in my heart that I would soon. And soon I did. Sooner than I ever dreamed. When I arrived home that night the light on my phone recorder was blinking. The message was from a friend, who at the time was the Chaplain for our local county hospital and he said, "Nancy, I was talking to the president of the hospital this week, and he remarked, 'We need to get more progressive around here. I would like to see us have a Labyrinth.' " + Dick told him that he knew someone who he thought would be interested in this project.

I contacted Mr. Shirk and told him I wanted to donate a Labyrinth to the hospital. He asked me to join a committee that was helping to plan a park at the hospital. I now had a place for my project. I had always known Spirit would take care of all.

March 26, 2001. The day after the workshop, I had

Heavenly Text

another vision of sacred geometry. I saw squares, circles, spirals, and then I saw a Labyrinth spiral. + An added affirmation. ("Thanks, God.")

April 28, 2001. I was in meditation when I heard, + *"We are going to anchor you. There will be some pain."* Then all of a sudden I felt a pain in the lower trunk of my body. I saw a circle and heard, + *"Male."* Then I felt another pain, saw another circle, and heard, + *"Female."* Then I felt another pain, saw another circle in the middle of the two circles and heard, + *"Holy Spirit."* Then I heard , + *"You are now anchored."* I then saw a Labyrinth. +

What an unusual experience, but I felt Spirit was conveying to me that they had anchored me, my male and female counterparts, and I would forever remain balanced.

I silently prayed, "Thanks. What a blessing. Harmony within. The Labyrinth must also be a symbol for the balance of the male and female. Are you reminding me that when we stick to the path we reach our goal? Are you also telling me the Labyrinth is a symbol of the path to the Divine? A symbol of death and rebirth? Are you telling me my life is unfolding like a Labyrinth? That this is a turning point in my life? Now that I've reached the center and found Christ within, will my life spiral back out?"

I knew Anne was to arrive in a few days and wondered if her coming had anything to do with this occurrence. I then heard, + *"Anne's trip is a gift for you."*

May 1, 2001. Anne arrived. Again, she had not been here for two years. It was a whirlwind three-day trip with many appointments and a beneficial one-day workshop for

Heavenly Text

CranioSacral workers. She began the workshop by saying, "I want you all to know this class is a gift. You will all be taken to a higher level of work." + (I had just heard that a few days prior.) She proceeded to teach us Hugh Milne's *"Windows to the Sky,"* which are main acupuncture points in the body. She, also, explained how pain is the window to our souls. (I recalled the experience of anchoring.) She also at one point explained that when we are balanced, the root chakra (red), and crown chakra (purple) become one, and "our contact with the heavens" is better. + (I immediately thought of my visions of red. The opening of my eighth chakra? Affirmation once again. "Thanks, God"). The workshop was a compelling day of learning and feeling the Spirit of God in many profound ways. I prayed for the wisdom to remember all and to be able to move forward with a deeper connection to Spirit.

Later when Anne and I were talking I told her that I was confused and wondered why I wasn't receiving as many visions as I did several years earlier. She put my mind at ease by saying, "When you were a child, weren't most of the books you read full of pictures? As you grew older there were less pictures and more words." I responded, "That makes perfect sense. My visions were followed by the messages from Jesus, and now I get both, just when needed. You always have a way of putting my mind at ease. Thanks for being God's little messenger once again."

On May 3, 2001. Anne and I were having lunch. She was to depart shortly. A van would be picking her up to take her to St. Louis for her return flight home. While eating on the screened porch we suddenly heard this thud, and looked to the deck. There lay two tiny birds - two little yellow finches. They had simultaneously hit the window. + (What are the

Heavenly Text

chances of that?) We went out and picked them up. Anne held them both in her hands, close to each other and to her heart, comforting the one who appeared to be alive but dazed. She was sharing her energy with them when she suddenly exclaimed, "Please put your hand on my eye. It's very painful." (She was picking up the injury from the bird. I've explained before how healers don't give energy but share in energy when doing healing work.) Anne said, "This is some kind of gift from Mother Mary. Right before lunch I noticed I was spotting blood, and it is not time for my monthly menstrual period. I believe it is a sign from Mary and has to do with Motherhood. These two little birds are representative of something important. Pay attention to messages from Mary in the near future. Right now, I feel this is also a healing gift for me." I knew Anne had discontinued wearing her glasses a year or so ago and was receiving healing energy. We were administering healing energy to the birds and her eye, when we heard the door bell. Her ride had arrived. Then suddenly, one bird flew out of her hand. She laid the other lifeless bird in the flowers and rushed to gather her belongings. After Anne left, I relived our experience all afternoon wondering of its entire significance. I buried the little dead finch among my flowers in the yard and I heard, + *"You too will rise and fly."*

("Thanks, God, I patiently wait for your guidance. I recalled the encounter with two huge butterflies when Anne was leaving my home back in April 1995.")

I recalled the previous two-way dream with Anne and how she had experienced a show of blood at that time. Some of the questions and thoughts that came to my mind: Is this experience once again telling me of a new spiritual initiation, a birthing? Is God again letting me know that Anne's healing hands, my healing hands, represent His blood going forth in

Heavenly Text

our world? Is this a message about the heart? Is He reminding me that in our healing work we share with His blood?

I also had another bird encounter while Anne was here. On May1st, the day Anne arrived, a bird kept coming to various windows in my house, going up and down the length of the windows. + Not just once, but over and over throughout the three days Anne was in town. I've written many bird stories and I could tell this bird was certainly trying to get my attention for its own story. For three days after Anne left, the bird was constantly scanning up and down my windows. I'd gone to different windows several times trying to communicate with the little brown bird with a yellow chest, but it always flew away. I didn't recognize the type of bird, so I looked it up in my new bird book. The best I could tell it was a Kingbird, which is not from this area. "He must be lost," I kept thinking to myself. Then on May 7, I was looking out my bedroom window when suddenly the bird came right up to the window only inches from me. The atmosphere that surrounded me became intense. With the bird's wings fluttering wildly, it flew up and down the length of the window several times and then flew back to a nearby branch. The bird then repeated this procedure to the window where I stood, and back to the branch at least a half a dozen times. My insides stirred with deep feelings of wonderment and joy. I kept asking, "What are you trying to tell me?" I internally heard, *"I want in."* + I asked, "How?" I heard +*"I want you to open your heart wider."* I was filled with Goosebumps as I carried on this mental telepathic conversation, remembering other times birds have delivered messages. I distinctly remembered the day on the deck just three days before. I also recalled the time I returned from visiting Conyers when a bird came to the window at the exact time I was reading the message, +*"Even a bird could be a sign*

Heavenly Text

from me." As I recalled the memory of the bird coming to my window seven years ago, I remembered that that bird had been brown with a yellow chest. I trembled inside as I prayed for insight, for understanding, for wisdom to comprehend what was transpiring. Is this from Mary? From Jesus?

Later, as I drove to church I was still talking to God and pleading for help in understanding the recent communications from nature. Then the Gospel reading at Mass was about listening to the Voice of God. + It felt like an answer.

I silently prayed, "Thanks God. Teach me, Lord, how to follow in Your ways, how to open my heart wider, so I can constantly hear the voices from the heavens. I can't help but think of St. Francis of Assisi and his communications with nature. I can't help but wonder what these messages represent. Are You going to dictate to me again? Is Mary going to dictate to me? I am amazed at the fact that Jesus the Christ is King, and You sent a Kingbird to get my attention. Please open my ears, my eyes, and my heart to continually hear Your words. Thanks, Thanks, Thanks."

May 6, 2001. Over the weekend a friend gave me several books to read, remarking at the time, "I haven't read these yet. Maybe you can see if they are any good." Since Erv was out of town, I spent the day reading *The Woman with the Alabaster Jar*, which is a story about Mary Magdelen. The author, Margaret Starbird, holds a master's degree in comparative literature. Starbird's theological beliefs were profoundly shaken when she read *Holy Blood, Holy Grail*, written by Baigent, Leigh, and Lincoln, a book that dared to suggest that Jesus Christ was married to Mary Magdelen and that their descendants carried on his holy bloodline in Western Europe. A Roman Catholic scholar, Starbird was shocked by such

Heavenly Text

heresy and set out to refute it, but instead found new and compelling evidence about Mary Magdelen, the same woman who anointed Jesus with precious unguent from her alabaster jar.

I found the book a fascinating read. I was intrigued beyond description in how this lady who had the letters b-i-r-d in her name might be describing what my bird experiences of the last week were symbolizing. First, I will briefly summarize her writings and make my comment afterwards.

Starbird drew her conclusions from an extensive study of history, heraldry, symbolism, medieval art, mythology, psychology, and the Bible. In brief, she explained how it is "plausible" that Mary Magdelen was the widow of Jesus, was taken by Joseph of Arimathea into hiding in France to protect her and her unborn child. She tells how a daughter was born to Mary Magdelen and was named Sarah. In Provence, France, where Mary Magdelen lived, there are numerous chapels, fountains, springs, and other geographical landmarks in the region that bear her name and her daughter's name.

Starbird wrote extensively on Christian history, the Dark Ages, the Inquisition, and how Christianity had many sects in the early church. The citizens of the region of Provence were called Cathars. They believed their version of Christianity to be both purer and older than orthodox Christianity, and closer to the teachings of Jesus and the Apostles. They claimed their church had retained the Holy Spirit conferred on the original Apostles which was passed on by the "laying-on-of-hands," the only ritual they regarded as authentic.

She writes that in 1209, the Vatican launched a crusade against the entire region of Provence, and Mary Magdelen; thus this flowering community of Mary Magdelen, who they called "Our Lady," was nipped in the bud. Every attempt was made

Heavenly Text
to blot the Cathars from memory. Perceiving the danger in allowing the rumor of Jesus' marriage and alleged bloodline to circulate, the Church of Rome moved quickly and firmly in the thirteenth century to ensure that the title "Our Lady" was referring to the Mother of Jesus (not the Wife of Jesus) who was to be venerated by the faithful. This was also the time in history when Catholics began honoring the Mother of Jesus.

The thoughts that swirled in my head connecting these new thoughts with my Spirit/energy work, the Labyrinth, and my mystical experiences intrigued me beyond description. My recent experiences with the symbols of blood and motherhood were foremost in my mind. Was the show of blood a sign for me to pay attention to the messages of Mary Magdelen that I was soon going be reading about? I believe so. I know I'm following in Jesus' teaching by doing "my Spirit/energy work, laying-on-of-hands." Was God once again using nature (the bird) to write His messages? I felt deep in my heart that I was being prompted to write this message in my writings.

I called Anne and told her of all my recent findings, further bird experiences, and my thoughts thinking I should write about them. She simply said, "Isn't God wonderful how He uses us all for His work? Spirit communicates to us the thoughts of time in many ways." I asked her if she had started her menstrual period and she said, "Oh, no, that definitely was a sign from above to get our attention." I reminded her of the previous time we had experienced a sign of blood to prompt my writings.

I am amazed and in awe at the ways of Spirit, and how I am gently nudged and guided. I know I keep better understanding the smallness and oneness of the universe. I am better understanding how it is possible for thoughts to be

Heavenly Text

reflected to us over eons of time to make sense of the order of the cosmos. I've read many times about the power of thought, how thoughts are matter, and how matter in turn attracts particles on the same vibratory level and continues to build. For me, intense thoughts with emotion are prayer. They are truths being spoken. Prayer is the language of God. Somehow, I have seemingly been able to tap into this universal language of words and of Light.

I believe this Spirit language is what my dream of hearing the word "*conceptual*" was conveying to me. Spirit can teach us visually, or with words, with thoughts, with nature, with dreams, or, in other words, with *concepts*. It's not a knowing but "conceptual." It's sensing the vibration of truth. Spirit can communicate to us by changes in reality that get our attention in order to convey the hidden truths. The Divine consciousness speaks to our human consciousness, offering insights and revelations. I believe we could also call this "the language of the soul." My bird experiences are one way, one *concept,* that Spirit uses to help me grow, to write and to evolve. I believe if we ask the questions, the answers come, in whatever way is the easiest for us to comprehend. It's none other than: "Ask and you shall receive." "Seek and you shall find. Knock and the door will be open to you."

I keep wondering though: Why haven't I heard this story of Jesus possibly being married to Mary Magdelen before? I certainly think I was told to write about it in a very poignant way. If the Catholic Church erred in days past, why can't they say they have made mistakes and enlighten everyone with information that has been lost over time? I'm sure there are many things hidden or lost in the Dark Ages of Christianity. I believe no religion or culture is without mistakes. We are all human. But to forgive and enlighten others is what growth is about. I believe it is time to search within every tradition and religion for their deeper wisdom, to learn to forgive and forget and move forward. It is time to unite the universal thoughts of God, the spoken truths over the eons of time, in order to create His Kingdom here on earth. For me, the coming of His Kingdom seems to be none other than the shift in our consciousness. **Christ will come again, within each one of us - one at a time.**

I wonder what other glorious messages the future will reveal. I just know that when a soul trusts God rather than self, God makes Himself understood. I know my religion is not a duty, but a way of life that has become an adventure. My life no longer seems to be in my hands. I just seem to flow with what is happening, flowing with the thoughts of Spirit directing me. I have learned that the purpose of living is to discover the purpose of living.

As I finished typing these last paragraphs, the mystery brown bird made a quick pecking trip to the window (here where I type), as if to say, "*Thank You*." + But I know I'm the one that needs to say, "Thank You, God, thank You. Continue to lead the way."

Months later in reading The Gospel of Philip in the Nag Hammadi texts, I read that Mary Magdelen was an intimate companion of Jesus. Did this mean physically or spiritually?

I also read three more highly researched books written by scholars and historians on the subject of Jesus' marriage and descendants: *The Messianic Legacy* written by the same authors as *Holy Blood, Holy Grail*, *The Hiram Key*, written by Knight and Lomos, and *Bloodline of the Holy Grail*, by Gadner. I found these books extremely interesting. Although

Heavenly Text

each author presents their information differently, they all wrote that Jesus was married. Whether they are right or not, all of these writings prove to me there is much more to our Christian history than we realize.

Then in 2008, I read *Love Without End by* Glenda Green, an excellent read. Glenda was the recipient of many messages from Jesus. Jesus told her that He and Mary Magdelen were not married but were very close friends. He also said her daughter Sarah was his constant delight and Sarah gave him an opportunity to foster special abilities and consciousness in a very young one. *Love Without End* is a marvelous read and I highly recommend it. I continue to wonder why I was instructed to write about Mary Magdelen, Jesus, and Sarah?

June 5, 2001. Another unusual occurrence happened with my friend and co-worker, Dottie H. She was at my home and we were exchanging Spirit/energy work. I had my hands on her head, and for some unknown reason I started silently wondering if I might have known Dottie in a previous life. She casually remarked something about seeing a tiny baby in her mind's eye. She then followed with the comment, "I guess by seeing a baby in my minds' eye Spirit is letting me know I'm just a baby at this work." I said this time out loud, "I wonder if we ever knew each other in another life?" She replied, "I've always thought there is a good possibility because I felt so drawn to you from the first day we met." Sometimes words seem to be put in my mouth and this was one of those times. I found myself stating, "You were probably a Ruth." + Having uttered those words, I chilled from head to toe. Dottie said, "What did you just do? I can't believe how I'm chilling and shaking from head to toe." I remarked, "I believe Spirit must be at work here. Do you suppose we've touched upon

Heavenly Text

something of the past?" She and I both kept feeling repeated chills, electrical sensations, from head to toe, wondering and questioning what was transpiring. She said, "We probably need to read Ruth in the Bible." Both our bodies over-reacted to that statement by tingling and chilling to a point of vibration. + A most profound mysterious moment.

I have learned over the years that when electrical sensations like this happen I need to pay close attention. I have learned that these sensations are my intuition letting me know, physically, what I already know subconsciously.

Then, when Dottie had her hands on me, she was directed to go to my feet. Holding my toes she said, "This is strange, I am seeing a dragonfly and a strange symbol. I wonder what this means?" +

When we were finished I opened my Bible to Ruth. We read together that Ruth had a baby named Obed, who was the grandfather of David. Dottie said, "I just saw a baby, could you have been my baby?" We laughed and chilled, and through tears and awe, I said, "I can hardly believe this. I just questioned in meditation a couple of days ago the possibility of my being in the bloodline of David. Isn't this too much? Spirit is a hoot how they keep toying with my emotions and conveying messages."

Then we looked up dragonfly in the *Animal Speak* book. It said, "Dragonflies are very ancient with estimates of having been around for 180 million years. It takes two years for the egg of a Dragonfly to develop into an adult." The book said, "If Dragonfly is in your life, look for change to occur. Dragonflies remind us that we are light and can reflect light in powerful ways. It brings the brightness of transformation." (Does this fit with my life, or what? Is Spirit trying to explain to me the growth of my soul from the beginning of time?)

Heavenly Text

Dottie was stunned and speechless. Our eyes widened in wonderment as we discussed the profoundness of it all. We marveled in how the series of messages pertained to us and my recent writings, wondering if it was possible that our souls were actually mother and daughter of long ago? Or was Spirit playing a game with us to get our attention? I also wondered if this was indicating to me that I'm reaching the culmination of a two-year period of transformation? Or do I have two more to go? Probably the latter, as there is no end - - we keep evolving. I also wondered if I was supposed to write about the occurrence? Did this happen to just add validity? This was definitely a topic to raise eyebrows for doubting-Thomas's not believing in reincarnation.

I filed the information in my heart and began praying about it, but Spirit seemed to keep pushing me to write. I couldn't get the thoughts out of my mind. I kept saying to myself, "You can always use the delete key down the road if it seems too bizarre for others."

When these things happen to me, they make sense at the time, but when I go to write about them, it often feels strange and I want to question my sanity. To write information that is conveyed by Spirit is a hard chore. Language doesn't seem to capture the moment. On an intellectual level, it's hard to understand and explain, but on an emotional level it feels comfortable and right. I guess that's what learning the concepts of God is all about. I'm glad there are witnesses to help me review and confirm. It's an amazing experience to be part of two realities.

June 18, 2001. Erv and I went to visit Mom. On the way we stopped in Louisville to visit my friend Jane. She had invited us to dinner. Jane and I had previously planned for us

Heavenly Text

to get together the next day for Spirit/energy work while Erv and my brother played golf. Jane asked me as soon as I arrived if it was OK if her friend Pat joined us the next morning. "Of course," I said, "Has she ever experienced healing work?" Jane replied, "No, but she called me this morning, full of excitement, and said she had had a mystical experience during the night. During the night, she heard her name called. She then saw light coming from her hands and was told she was to learn to use her hands in healing. I told her it was perfect because you were coming today. Isn't Spirit's timing something?" + I smiled inside and thanked God for the upcoming opportunity and privilege.

The next morning when the three of us met at Pat's home we immediately all felt a deep presence of God. I asked Pat to tell me what happened the night before and asked if she had ever had any other mystical experiences. "Oh, yes!" she exclaimed, "By far the most wonderful was last year on September 14 when Jesus appeared to me." + I'm sure my eyes widened, my heart was swelling, as I exclaimed, "September 14 was the birthday of my daughter, Pam, who died eighteen years ago." Pat went on to say, "Jesus just appeared, right there on those steps, and began talking to me. I didn't hear audible words, it was telepathic, but I understood everything He said. He told me he wanted me to use my hands in healing work. I was naturally surprised and somewhat frightened. He told me not to be afraid and that He would send someone to teach me. Now, I'm thinking it must be you. When Jesus appeared to me He told me many things. It took me two hours afterwards to write down all of the conversation. I haven't done anything about learning healing work and didn't really know how to begin. Then, night before last, I was awakened and saw hands of light and heard the message again. That's

Heavenly Text

when I called Jane. I'm amazed that you're here. I believe Jesus sent you to teach me how to do His healing work."

I tried to explain how I've been guided by Spirit for over seven years learning healing work. We talked for some time and then I had Pat lie on my massage table. I showed her how Spirit uses me as a vessel. At one point Pat remarked, "When my eyes are closed, I keep seeing a butterfly." Jane immediately spoke up and said, "Pat, remember how the three butterflies kept hovering around us on my deck Sunday night? How they kept landing on us and remained for so long." I spoke up and said, "Pam loved butterflies and we even had a banner at her funeral with a huge butterfly on it that said, 'Butterflies are Free.' It's how I envisioned her after she died." Jane commented, "There are three of us here now and we had the encounter with the three butterflies the other night. This is almost spooky." I responded, "Jane, not spooky, but wonderful. Do you remember the first time you called me was back in 1995? You had read my book about Pam and wanted me to come to speak at the University to your medical students. It was also on September 14th that you called. Lots of coincidences here with Pam. + Also the first time Anne was at my house, two butterflies appeared out of nowhere at night when we were sitting on my porch. Interesting huh? Isn't Spirit fun? It always seems like a game, piecing the puzzle together."

I explained to Jane and Pat how I had just recently written about how dying to self is like a cocoon dying so a butterfly can emerge. We all chilled over and over marveling at the ways of Spirit. We exchanged phone numbers and e-mails and I told Pat I would plan to spend time with her the next time I came to Kentucky.

When at Mom's I also did Spirit/energy work on her. She

Heavenly Text

slept through most of the procedure, but her body reacted in a dramatic way. She did surprise me by saying, "Nancy I think I'm supposed to tell you that I now live in two worlds." I asked her what she meant and she said, "I can't explain it but at times I'm somewhere else. It's different and I just can't explain it." In my heart I knew God was educating her, preparing her for the transition into another reality, and He wanted me to know that. I know that when one steps into another reality it's called enlightenment or awakening or self-realization. Each soul goes through this one way or another. As I processed what was going on with her, it entered my awareness that since mankind is evolving into a higher state of consciousness, it seems logical to me that the elder generation are transitioning at an accelerated rate in their sub-conscious (Alzheimer's?) to make room for the new younger generations of higher evolved minds. As mankind evolves into this higher consciousness, balance and counter balance has to take place everywhere. We are all involved in the co-creation of mankind - it's part of God's greater plan.

As I typed the above experiences from Kentucky into my computer the mystery brown and yellow bird kept going up and down my window. + ("Thanks, God. I'm thrilled to be working for You, on an on-going basis. My heart swells with constant joy knowing You are leading the way.")

August 4, 2001. My birthday. I turned sixty years old and some wonderful friends had an exceptional party for me. Some would call the gathering of women a "croning," but I call it the day God spoke to me through others.

The hostess began with an explanation of the meaning of crones -- wise women-- and explained how it used to be a

Heavenly Text

custom to honor the elder women in a community. She explained how cronings are again being held throughout the country in an effort to resume this practice. (Something new to me. I had never heard of a croning.) Then each present gave me a personal tribute.

The ceremony of love ended with me kneeling in the middle of the room as all placed their hands on me and said a prayer in unison. A very profound nurturing, loving experience.

I also received material gifts, but nothing compared to the love I felt from those present. The day will forever remain locked in my heart, as the day God let me witness His presence in each one of these women. It was very beautiful. I would compare it to a living funeral, a testimony, that one never hears. I felt exceptionally blessed.

("Thanks God my heart swells with joy.)

September 11, 2001. This day will go down in history as a terrible day of tragedy, the day the World Trade Center towers fell in New York. Much will be written about this horrific destruction of lives and property. I will only say that I spent most of the day praying and meditating. I recalled the vision I had seen of this happening back in 1996. I kept hearing throughout the day, + *"Stay calm, hold peace in your heart."* I asked Jesus if there was anything He wanted me to write.

I heard, +*"Tell my people that the world needs to come into balance. Without love and understanding this will not be possible. What the world witnessed today is what can happen worldwide if love does not prevail. There is an urgent need to unite our hearts and minds for the greater good. I surround my people with love. They in turn need to surround each other with this loving presence. Nothing survives on its own; all is*

Heavenly Text
connected to Me. I am reaching out to the people of the world to help balance the planet earth. Mankind's thoughts create his reality, thoughts of love will create love, thoughts of war will only bring more sorrow and hurt. Unite my people and become one with Me."

September 13, 2001. A new individual, Lisa C., came into my life. I met her through a friend. She is another individual who has the gift of seeing inside the body (medical intuitive) and receiving symbolic spiritual messages from Spirit. When we got together to share, she first scanned my body to check my health. She immediately said, "You are very healthy. You are definitely on your correct path. I see you bouncing along, enthusiastically trying to get others to join you." She suddenly said, "This is very interesting, it's the first time I've ever seen this before. Your hypothalamus is a flame. It's a red and purple flame." + I chilled, silently thanking God for the affirmation and replied, "Thanks, for that information. I believe Spirit is just letting us know that my eighth chakra is open. I've just recently written about that." She went on to say, "You're very healthy, except I see blinders over your eyes. + I wonder what that is about?" (All I could think of was how M.L. had told me not once, but twice, that Jesus had placed something over my eyes, so that I would only write what He showed me.) Through tears I said, "God is so good. That information has been given to me twice before and you knew nothing about it. What an affirmation. Not only do I know that God is affirming what I've heard before, but He's letting me know you are a gift to me from Him. Your gifts of knowing and seeing will report messages to me. You have an amazing gift and I know without a doubt God is blessing me with your presence. I just love it when I get two-way messages like this. Isn't this wonderful? "

Heavenly Text

I was jumping inside with joy knowing that I now had another direct line from God. I realized it was the 13th, Mary's day, and I considered the experience a gift from her. ("Thanks, God.")

September 15, 2001. Megan, the daughter of a friend of mind came to see me. Megan has lived in Arizona and was now living in Kansas City. I hadn't seen her for nearly twenty years. She had heard from her mom that I was doing healing work, and she had come hoping to learn from me. Before we began, she shocked me by saying, "Nancy, I've never had a chance to tell you how much I enjoyed the book you wrote about Pam. I thought you might be interested in knowing that Pam came to me in a dream the night she died." I chilled + as I heard the following, "I dreamed of Pam and knew she had died. In the morning I told Mom I thought she should call you to see how Pam was. She did and you told her Pam had died during the night. I've never forgotten that and still to this day often think of Pam. She was so much fun when we were growing up." Stunned I replied, "I guess Pam knew that you were going to be coming here one of these days. I know she often brings me students to learn healing work. For instance, just last week, a friend of Pam's, whom I've never met before (from her junior high school days) called and asked for a copy of my book. She asked, 'Have you written any more and what are you up to these days?' After I shared with her, she made an appointment and came to see me. She, too, wants to learn God's healing energy work. It seems Pam is definitely busy from the heavens."

September 19, 2001. Lisa and I got together again. When she had her hands on me she began to speak, + "This has never

Heavenly Text

happened to me before. I'm seeing Mary, the Mother of Jesus, I've not previously seen her. She is carrying something in her hand. I now see her placing a heart over your heart. It's unusual, it's a heart with a crown, and a cross, and a flame, and I'm hearing **'The Sacred Heart of Jesus.'** She is also covering you, no, both of us, with what looks like a blue mantle."

I was shedding tears with joy and thanks, saying nothing to interrupt Lisa's deep meditative state. She continued with, + "I see what appears to be a cord going from your heart to your hypothalamus. And there it is again, the flame again. Your hypothalamus is a flame. I also see a cord coming out the top of your head going up to the heavens. Isn't this interesting! I also am hearing, *"Tell her she is on her correct path. She has a very important job."* Do you know what an Essene is? (Essene's were a religious sect in Jesus' time. Many believe Jesus was an Essene). I'm being told you were one. Oh, we both were one, in an earlier life." During all of her visual and verbal information I kept hearing within the words, +*"I'm in you, You're in Me."*

Needless to say we talked for a lengthy time afterwards. I told her about having a vision years ago, in which Jesus showed me His Sacred Heart. (Lisa is not a Catholic and asked what Sacred Heart meant.) I said, "I wrote back then that the symbol was probably the idea of some artists. After today I seriously doubt that, and I have an intense need to find out what the deeper meaning is. I'm wondering why this symbol again, and I'm wondering why it is being conveyed to me in this manner?"

Later, I looked through my past writings and discovered that it was in 1994 that I was shown Jesus' Sacred Heart in a vision. It was Christmas time. At that time, I was dealing with thoughts of death, wondering if God was telling me I was

Heavenly Text

going to die or if was I dying to an old way of life. I had, at that time, written in my manuscript, (which I'd since forgotten) a message about the Sacred Heart that Mariamante, a visonary had received from Jesus; + *"The Bridegroom calls His brides to Him; come and dwell with Me. Make my Heart your abode. Stay with Me in love; never leave Me. Think of Me always and I will dwell within you perpetually. I am in you and you in Me and together you will dwell in the Trinity, as the Father has promised me. Be at peace. You have come home."*

I remembered how those words had affected me then and even more so now. I now believe Jesus was inviting me and telling me that I was on my way to becoming one with Him. He was trying to show me the way by showing me the symbol of His Sacred Heart. Now it's years later and I just swell with joy knowing I'm following in what He wants me to do. Holding Him in our hearts is what He wants each of us to do. It has taken me seven years and now I heard the words from Him. I recall the intuitive message from the mystery bird, *"I want you to open your heart wider."* It has taken me seven years and now I heard the words from Him. +*"I'm in you, You're in Me."*

("Thanks, God, I'm overwhelmed with joy. I believe I must be doing what you requested.)

Then, later that day in meditation, I seemed to come to an inner-knowing, an understanding, that the imagine of the Sacred Heart represented the uniting of the heart chakra with the crown chakra. I was told, +*"When a person is in balance, and the chakras come together (through Kundalini), the flame of the Holy Spirit will overshadow them, and that one will have a better connection with the heavens."*

I had a powerful feeling of having discovered a deep secret. The Sacred Heart was a symbol for transcendence. + If

Heavenly Text

this is true, I thought the symbol of the Sacred Heart is the most important message of all times for all of mankind. Christ is showing us His Heart and in doing so is showing us that life is about bringing ourselves into balance as He did. The Sacred Heart is more than a symbol of His love, it is the **power** of His love. He's showing us how the heart chakra and crown chakra need to unite. He is showing us His Heart inviting us to become one with Him by balancing our heart and crown chakras.

The information seemed to be calling me to write more about this. I felt I was being led to bring the pieces of the pie together to make a unified sense of it all. I wondered how I could trace the history of the symbol of the Sacred Heart. The next day I asked Father Charlie where the symbol of the Sacred Heart originated. He answered, "I've always heard the church claimed that the symbol of the Sacred Heart began with a vision Saint Margaret Alacoque had in the seventeenth century. After her vision she started the devotion to the Sacred Heart." (I made a mental note to read her life story.)

I also researched and found some books on symbols. The following is a collection of some of my findings. The symbol of the Sacred Heart appeared in a number of stained glass windows several centuries before the seventeenth century (so before St. Margaret Alacoque). I discovered that the heart as a symbol of the soul was very commonplace in Christian iconography. I discovered the cross was used as a symbol in many and varying ways. Native Americans believe the cross is a symbol of the union of cosmic forces, the coming together of polarities which create the world. A cross can sometimes be defined as a Vortex, an intersection of angles, which marks where pairs come together to form a power spot. A red cross was used by the underground church, after the inquisition, as a

Heavenly Text

sexual symbol, the uniting of the male and female. The cross was also used by many in ancient times as a symbol of truth and enlightenment. For Christians, the cross symbolizes the crucifixion. The crown of thorns has been used as a symbol of Christ ever since the crucifixion.

Thoughts swirled in my mind. I ask, didn't Jesus come to show us the way? Isn't the crucifixion of Jesus (on the cross) a symbol to remind Christians to become one with Him by baring our sufferings in the name of God? To learn to surrender to the will of God? Didn't Jesus say become like Me? Hasn't Jesus been trying to explain the importance of understanding the cross, the importance of evolving into a higher consciousness, the importance of resurrection and ascension to us over the years in many, many ways and through many symbols? Is He doing the same with the symbol of the Sacred Heart, containing a cross, crown, and flame? Is uniting the male and female our purpose in life? I believe so.

October 8, 2001. I visited my friend, Anjail, who shared Spirit/energy work with me. Although legally blind, she too has spiritual sight. For sometime now, she too, sees Mary when working with me. She said, "I see Mother Mary. She is here and she is placing a triangle, full of light, at your heart. I wonder what this means?" + Again, my tears began to flow. I whispered, "I wish I could see with spiritual sight. I wonder how much longer before the blinders are lifted from my eyes?" Then I thought of Anjail who can't physically see and was ashamed. Anjail continued to give a description of what she was seeing. "There's beautiful Light. + She is covering you with beautiful Light. I see lots of gold and green surrounding you."

Our time together was overwhelming me with joy. I don't

Heavenly Text

recall all that transpired but I know I felt a deep presence of love. Later when Anjail and I talked, I shared with her my previous heart experience with Lisa. Then I said, "Isn't Spirit wonderful how they are guiding me to write about the evolution of mankind? I feel so privileged to share in this work. I wonder when and how this will all come to fruition. I'm sorry I complained about not having spiritual sight, when you cannot see this reality. Please forgive me."

As if on cue, another couple of books arrived in my life, *The Ancient Secrets of the Flower of Life* by Drunvalo Melchizedek. The person who brought them to me said, "Father Mike suggested I come to talk to you six years ago but I'm just now getting up the courage. Father Mike said that you might be able to help me. I've had some unusual mystical experiences." We had talked for over an hour when she opened her backpack and said, "I brought these books. They are my brother's. I have read them and thought you might enjoy them." Thinking she must be psychic, I assured her it was the exactly the right time. I explained that I had been reading and writing about the Flower of Life from the internet. Needless to say I was thrilled. And all I could say was, "Isn't God's timing a hoot? This one took six years. Spirit sure shuffles things around on schedule. Has Mike read these?" She said, "Oh, No. I just got them recently."

Drunvalo gave an in-depth history of sacred geometry and physics, with the geometry of light in all of creation. He explained, with evidence, the relationship of all energy throughout creation-how we are all linked together. He described the very complex and complicated way the energy system works in the body.

Drunvalo gave a lengthy history about Egypt, because the

Heavenly Text

Egyptians knew the importance of sexual energy and human orgasm (Kundalini) and that they believed balancing the chakras was the key to eternal life. He illustrated how Kundalini realigns the nervous system, which allows us to experience new levels of awareness.

He also stated that when the right brain and left brain balance, one is moving into unity consciousness, which some would call enlightenment.

Each book I read seems to more clearly explain our species' evolution into the higher consciousness that is transpiring at this time in history. I know we can learn to participate in this process. We can accelerate this process individually, if we so desire. Drunvalo's book helped to reaffirm my message about the Sacred Heart.

I was also reading *Keeper of the Secrets* by Robert Siblerud about the ancient secrets of mystical societies. Siblerud wrote about the Shamans, Druids, Essenes, Gnostics, Kabbalists, Hermetics, Alchemists, Magicians, Witches, Sufism, Rosicrutions, and Freemasons, which all splintered from early Christian beliefs. All of these groups believed they did everything in the name of God. The author gave a brief history of how these mystical societies have passed symbols and traditions down through the years. He also explained the symbols of sacred geometry, the tetrahedron (The Star of David), the Tree of Life, and other Jewish Symbols.

Symbolic art is nothing new. Many thousands of years ago, primal cultures used pictures and pictographs on cave walls to represent ideas relating to life and death. Mankind has sought revelation through signs and symbols throughout all of creation. I am realizing I could spend years researching symbols, but I'd found enough to convince me that since

Heavenly Text

ancient times symbols have been used to help man's logical minds grasp truths that are beyond ordinary reality. It's clear to me that the alchemists, hounded by the Inquisition, were careful to hide their faith behind symbols.

I believe my message in meditation about the Sacred Heart was right on target. I believe the church adopted the symbol of the heart and crown and called it the Sacred Heart, not realizing its true significance. When St. Margaret started the devotions for the Scared Heart, she was not fortunate enough to have the information that is now available. When I read writings about her, I discovered that she had a difficult time with the clergy not believing in her visions. It was not until many years later that the Church decided she was not hallucinating.

I know first hand how this problem still remains. It's why I spend my time trying to add confirmation and affirmation of God's ways. Changing our thoughts on reality and understanding Spirit are very hard for many to comprehend, especially since we've always been told and taught differently.

Isn't it interesting how, throughout time, much has become overlapped, confused, and misinterpreted? I question many teachings and have many misgivings about many teachings of my religion, but I know God leads the way for us, no matter where we are or what faith we embrace. I believe there is Divine Order in the unfolding of creation. Numerous thoughts continue to run through my mind as I try to comprehend and understand all. I do know that throughout life much has been done by others, some knowingly, others unknowingly, that has effected us all. ("Thanks, God. I wonder if someday there will be a list of all the multitude of discrepancies?")

In my research on symbols, I also read more about the triangle and the pyramid. The symbol of the trinity is a

Heavenly Text

universal symbol of light given to us down through the ages, in many ways from many religions. I learned the triangle was the ancient symbol for the Goddess. More than once I read that the triangle is also the symbol of the Soul, which appears when Divine understanding is reached. I found that the triangle in early Christianity was the symbol of the Trinity. Jesus possessed Divine understanding, and that is the reason the double triangle, the tetrahedron, became the symbol for the Star of David. The Greek word for pyramid is Spirit, light, or fire. I read that the pyramid structures in Egypt and elsewhere are symbols of our connection with Spirit. The pyramid in Egypt is thought by many to be the source of all energy connecting the earth and heavens. Much has been written about the Great Pyramid of Giza and how it contains all spiritual and mathematical knowledge within its structure.

I now know, without a doubt, that we are all of light, evolving into higher beings of Light. We have just forgotten over time that this is our purpose for being here on earth. Even our forefathers placed a pyramid, with a single eye on the dollar bill. I now understand that this ancient symbol was passed down from the early Freemasons who felt the symbol represented the Sacred Coming of Christ - who was regarded as the Chief Cornerstone. Did our forefathers also possess a knowledge of symbols that has been lost with time? Was this their way to remind us that our nation was not only founded under God but that it's possible to become beings of Light? Doesn't it say in the Bible, "If the eye is single the whole body is full of light?"

I am now very confident that my video vision of a year ago was telling me that I have connected with my Higher

Heavenly Text

self, connected with Spirit on a different level, that my eighth chakra is open, and I AM one with God. I believe this step in evolution is a major one. I believe this is what is meant by being born again. Being born again is not just about Baptism or accepting Christ as our Lord and Savior. It's about bringing our entire being into union with God, mentally, physically and spiritually. It's about being cleansed by the Holy Spirit. It's about being the temple of God. It's about love. It's about connecting our heart with Christ. It's about understanding that I AM in partnership with God. It's about finding Christ within. The audible voice I heard, the vision of the Light hovering on top of the Pyramid, seeing the dove, were profound messages from heaven. Then the placing of the Sacred Heart and the triangle, by Mother Mary, finalized this message for me. I have balanced the male and female. I know I AM now one with God. I have awakened to the knowledge that we are all one with God, always have been, and always will be. It is time for mankind to understand this.

("Thanks, God, for all of the affirmations on this. My heart swells until I feel it could explode.")

December 4, 2001. A new individual, Paula, came into my life. A friend of mind who lives in St. Louis, had suggested she come to see me. Immediately upon meeting, Paula began sharing with me spiritual experiences she was having. She was relieved to find out that she was not alone. She had never met anyone who could explain to her what was happening in her life. Paula shared with me that Jesus had appeared to her several times as the Infant Jesus of Prague. It had frightened her and she knew no one to share the information with who would not make fun of her. It was a joy

Heavenly Text

to see her cry through tears of sadness and joy, knowing God had brought us together.

December 7, 2001. I came home to find a package on my front porch. I was in charge of a recycle Christmas sale for our parish, so I presumed the box contained Christmas decorations. As I picked up the box I found a note. I immediately realized that God was at work when I read. "Nancy, This statue of the Infant Jesus of Prague is very old and I don't know if you can use it or not. The rest are a few Christmas decorations." +

Now, what are the chances of that happening, just three days after my hearing of the Infant Jesus of Prague from Paula? I immediately called my friend who brought the box and asked her if it was all right to give the statue to someone who would really appreciate it. She explained to me that the statue belonged to her grandmother, then her mother, and when she was recently clearing out her mother's home, she had brought it to her home. She knew she would never use it. She was happy I had found the perfect home.

December 10, 2001. I spent a long time meditating before getting out of bed. When I did get up I had a supreme gift. I was in my bathroom when I heard a vibrating sound. I couldn't imagine where is was coming from. I went toward some glass shelves and realized the sound was coming from a statue of Mother Mary. The statue of Mary was literally vibrating on the shelf. + Nothing else on this shelf was moving or vibrating. I thought I must be imagining this so I picked the statue up and the noise stopped immediately. I asked Mary, "Are you trying to speak to me?" I put the statue down and on two shelves above, another ceramic piece, which is of the face of Mary began to vibrate. Now, I became very agitated and began to

Heavenly Text

cry, exclaiming, "What are you trying to tell me?" I picked this piece up and the vibrating noise again stopped immediately. I was perplexed, mystified and thrilled all at the same time. I thanked Mary as I cried and wondered what message was being conveyed.

Shortly, the phone rang. When I picked it up, it was Paula, timidly asking if she was calling too early, and could she please come by on her way to school? (Paula is getting her masters in art at the University.) I usually don't like to take appointments as early as she wanted to come, but I could tell in her voice she was desperate. Plus, I knew I wanted to give her the gift of the statue of the Infant Jesus, so I said nothing except, "Sure that will be fine."

When she arrived and we went upstairs, I immediately handed her the box with the statue in it. When she opened it, she was stunned and for a time speechless. "You don't know how much this means to me," she said through tears, "I just had a huge argument with God and told Him I didn't want to be part of His mystic happenings any more unless He showed me a sign. And here it is. Where did you get this?" She explained that she was angry because her art class critique had not gone well the day before. No one had said anything about her work. She had painted from her heart and placed the Infant Jesus of Prague statue in several of her paintings. No one commented on her work, good or bad. It had crushed her. She didn't understand. I said, "I bet they were just stunned and didn't know what to say. Anyway, you at least now know that Jesus and Mary approve." I explained the earlier vibrating statues of Mary which preceded her phone call. We laughed and cried through tears of joy knowing we were in good hands with Spirit communicating to each of us.

("Thanks, God. Thanks, Mary. What a joy to work with

Heavenly Text

you.")

December 25, 2001. We had already celebrated Christmas with our family at Thanksgiving because Deanna and Jeff would be with his family this year on Christmas Day, so it was a relaxed month. I realized how hectic I've let the holidays become in my life.

Christmas morning, Erv and I went to 9am Mass. During Mass I heard, +*"You need to write one page summarizing your writings of this last year. Simple enough for a child to understand. Call it, "What All Need to Know."*

I prayed, "Now, how am I supposed to do that? What a challenge you have offered me God. I hope I can accomplish what You ask."

December 27, 2001. I went to my computer and tried to obey the request. I knew it had taken me sixty years, but I now better understood the bigger picture of life. The mysteries of the universe have been revealed to me through many avenues. My prior narrow view had expanded into a knowingness that I wanted to share with the world.

It took me several days, but with the help of Spirit, I accomplished what I thought at first would be impossible. I wrote What All Need To Know.

I prayed, "God, I hope this is what you wanted. Please give me a sign of confirmation. Thanks for your trust in me. Is this what the vision of the big-book little-book was about? Do you want me to condense all the writings that have accumulated over the years? Or are we working on a children's book? Or both?" (Later I decided to use this as part of the introduction to my books and I put it on my web site.)

Heavenly Text

December 31, 2001. While meditating I saw a couple of flame letters - fire script. + I remembered previously reading about these. I have read that flame letters are a geometric code for the expansion of human consciousness. "Thanks, God, I'm overwhelmed. Is this the sign I asked for? Is this your language? Will I ever totally understand?"

Father Charlie told me shortly after Christmas, that while on vacation, he had read my manuscript. I told him I had continued to write and asked if he'd like to read more. I also told him I had been told at Mass on Christmas to condense all I knew to be true to one page. He replied, "Then I'll just read the one page."

When I gave him the one page he asked no questions and there was no discussion. I feel he is perplexed about my occurrences and prefers not to get involved. I don't know what his thoughts are because he is noncommittal. He did, however, help the situation here at home, because he told Erv that everything he read in (Vol. I & Vol. II) were in keeping with the teachings of the Catholic Church. (That was big! Thanks, God. Maybe Charlie's sole purpose is to help Erv feel more comfortable.)

February 23, 2002. A wonderful treat. Anne came to town for a few days. She took appointments and had another workshop. I had been teaching individuals and wanted her to also add her expertise.

When it came time for her to leave, she told me she wouldn't be back because her leadership wasn't needed here anymore. Deep inside I had known this day would come.

I shed tears of loss but tears of happiness knowing I'd come a long way. No one will ever know the gratitude I feel

Heavenly Text

for her guidance. In the last ten years I have learned a lifetime of knowledge. I am feeling more at peace all of the time. I have discovered my faith is not a religion but the belief I hold in my heart. I know I am one with God.

February 27, 2002. I received a gift. A screech owl took up residence at our home. + It arrived the morning after the night of the full moon. It lived in an old birdhouse, the one Erv put up years ago for the flicker woodpeckers, directly behind our home where I see it daily. Daily the owl stretched its head out the hole of the birdhouse and was clearly visibly sunning itself as it slept off and on throughout the day. At times I would sit and watch and it would open its eyes and stare at me. It remained for seven days and then it was gone. Three days later it returned for only one day and then we never saw it again. (I wondered of the significance of the number of days "7-3-1." I know that in numerology 11 is a very significant number.)

My *Animal Speak* book says the owl is the bird of magic, prophecy and wisdom. It says, "If a screech owl shows up, know it can stir your imagination, and heighten your sixth sense. Owls have a stimulating effect upon all energy and its medicine is powerful day and night." I remembered the owl in my cedar tree dream. Thanks, God."

March 23, 2002. I had a powerful prophetic dream. I was in a room with many individuals. I saw a huge mirror with my name printed across it. I was told to wear the mirror. I insisted it was too big. Then I heard someone say, + *"We'll make you a gold medallion to wear instead."* I then saw a medallion with my initials clearly engraved on it. An individual then placed the medallion around my neck. I was told to wear it with pride

Heavenly Text

and that there were few like this.

This dream was a huge affirmation. I've known for some time that I have mirrored others' problems in my body. Often hours before a client arrives I know of their problem - I feel it in my body. I believe this mirroring occurs so that a balance is created and then, when I share Spirit/energy work, healings can occur.

Gregg Braden, scientist and author of many books, who considers himself a bridge between science and spirituality, explains mirroring scientifically when he writes, "Please consider the following: When two electronic modules are placed near one another, with one vibrating quicker than the second, something interesting begins to happen. The module of lower frequency will have a tendency to match, through resonance, that of the higher pitch. This process is identical to that of the human energy system, which may be considered a module of composite frequencies reflecting individual cell and organ complexes. This module, our mind-spirit-body complex, when placed within the fields of another module (planetary or man) will have a tendency to move into resonance with the higher vibration. In the human energy system, the process takes on an additional component; the willingness of the conscious mind governing the body to adapt to the new range of vibration. The primary tool of adaptation is life itself, complete with the bundle of emotion, attitudes, perceptions, fears, and beliefs that provide the framework for the challenges of life. One key factor in this process is the willingness of the individual to achieve balance within the energetic system using the tools of Choice and Free Will. These are basic tools used to release old patterns of belief, lifestyle or relationships and adapt to new, more balanced patterns. When accomplished

Heavenly Text

successfully, this process is termed "healing" and a being is said to have "learned." The ancients taught meditative techniques to bypass the logical mind in an effort to consciously feel these vibrations as well as sense the pulses of Light." This quote is from his book *Awakening to Zero Point*.

April 15, 2002. + I had a vision of me sitting in front of a computer. There was a wastebasket by the side of my chair overflowing with papers in and around it. Were these pages from my manuscript? I knew I was being told to condense all my writings.

April 30, 2002. + In a vision I saw a map of the United States. The picture of the U.S. was upright then it suddenly fell backwards. The feelings I felt were not good. I shuddered thinking of its deeper meaning.

May 15, 2002. I got together with Paola who was here visiting her brother-in-law. She now lives in California but has lived many places throughout the world, including Italy and South America. She speaks several languages, is very knowledgeable, and a joy to be with. We had previously met several months before when she came to visit family here in Columbia. Back then when we discovered that we both did healing work we exchanged sessions. On this trip when she was on my table she remarked, "This is something that has never happened to me. I don't normally see pictures and I am seeing a very clear picture of two young children - it's you and me. We are dressed in white robes and are wearing sandals. I'm being made aware that we were sisters in another lifetime. Your name was Ann." We were discussing this powerful information at length when she suddenly said, "I'm now being told I'm supposed to make a pilgrimage. I'm to prepare to walk

Heavenly Text

the El Camino in Spain." I answered, "You'll have to walk it for both of us because I know I'll never do that. Maybe we could meditate everyday at the same time and see if we can connect. We could send energy around the world." She agreed, "That would be delightful." (Little did I know what our thoughts were manifesting at the time.)

May 24, 2002. + As I began seeing Light in a vision I also felt many sensations in my body. Then I saw a jigsaw puzzle box, and on the cover of the box I could see steps. The vision became clearer and I realized the steps were the steps on a pyramid. The top, the capstone, or the apex, of the pyramid was missing.

I felt the message was explaining, *"As you grow step by step, even though you don't see Me (the capstone), I am always with you."* Possibly an affirmation telling me why I saw the capstone of the pyramid in my lengthy vision years ago. Or was this an affirmation that I had pieced the pieces of the puzzle together?

May 31, 2002. I was awakened with a very strong lightning strike. + The only way to describe it is that it felt extremely wide.

When I went to church that day, I discovered it was a feast day of Mary, the Visitation, and I thought, "How perfect. I must have received grace from Mary earlier today." Then when I came home from church, a lone purple iris was blooming in front of the statue of Mary which I have in my front yard. This was very unusual because none of my irises have bloomed there for several years and this iris really stood out. I thanked Mary for the gifts. (No other Iris bloomed there the entire summer.)

Heavenly Text

June 8, 2002. I was awakened with a lightning jolt, and it felt like a needle or a pin was pricking my ear. I heard, "*Hear me with your pen. I'm in you.*"

I decided I was definitely being told to write more. I recalled the visions of the wastebasket of trash paper, the vision of the big book and little book that I had received over a year ago, and the message to condense all I know to be true to one page. The message was clear that it was time to condense my stack of over a thousand pages into a readable book. I began on what seemed a monumental task – my volume of books. How would I ever find the time?

June 14, 2002. A person on my table receiving Spirit/energy work said, "I see Mother Mary, she wants me to give you a message." + I was thrilled. "She is telling me she is proud of you working within the Catholic Church. She is proud of you and your plans to build the Labyrinth. I see her standing in the middle of a Labyrinth and water is coming out her feet--running out over the Labyrinth. She is now asking me to give you my favorite picture of her, but I don't want to." I commented, "That's fine. You don't have to. Where did you get the picture?" The person remarked, "My aunt brought it to me from Medjugore. I've had it in my prayer book for years." We then smelled the scent of roses. Another person was in the room and also smelled the roses. Powerful moments!

Later that day an envelope arrived at my home containing the slightly tattered and torn picture. When I saw the intensity of the beauty of the picture of Mary, I was thrilled to be the recipient of such a gift. My knees went weak as I read the note attached, "Thank you, you will see me," Mary.

I immediately went to Kinkos and had extra laminated copies made. I returned a copy to the sender. My original

Heavenly Text

copy is framed and is placed by my computer. It gives me strength. ("Thanks, Mary.")

June 20, 2002. In a vision I seem to be in the midst of a green mist surrounding the earth. + I didn't understand what this was about. It felt good. I'm sure time will tell.

June 24, 2002. + An intriguing dream. I was walking by a huge parish complex, a church, a rectory, a school. As I walked on the property I saw a huge concrete angel statue. As I passed, it came to life and began to walk with me. + The angel went into the rectory door. Almost instantly the angel came back out on the porch and cried out "Help me!" "Help me!" I asked, "Is this another priest's message?" End of dream.

Later that day when I returned home from noon Mass, a hawk was sitting on my deck. + It remained there for over three hours. Its presence felt very special. I know hawks are messengers from God and I considered this visit a huge thank you for starting to condense my writings. (The hawk has remained and become a permanent resident on our property. I see it often. What a gift!)

July 10, 2002. + In a vision I saw a being of Light holding my hands. I knew it was Jesus. He then laid His head on my feet. I asked, "Why this?" I heard nothing.

July 16, 2002. + In a vision I saw a bear gracefully falling out of a tree. I knew the bear had been put there as a baby and was now grown. The bear gracefully fell to the ground and began to play, joyfully bouncing about and rolling around.

Was this vision telling me I was going to fall from a tree? Why? I know a tree can be a symbol of growth and wisdom,

Heavenly Text
linking the earth and heavens. A bear is a symbol for going within to find answers. Lots for me to ponder on.

July 21, 2002. + I was awakened by a strange noise. In a vision I saw a tree. The wind was blowing hard and I saw a man gesture with a hand and the tree became full of Light. Then another gesture with a hand the tree instantly disappeared in flames. Why another tree dream? I've had so many tree dreams during my education and now two in a row. I know fire changes things from one state to another. Am I going to be going through a purification? I know fire renews nature. I recalled, "The wind blows wherever it pleases; you hear its sound, but you cannot tell where it comes from or where it is going. That is how it is with all who are born of the Spirit." (John 3:7-9)

July 23, 2002. Lisa and I were exchanging Spirit/energy work. She said she saw Mother Mary who was showing her that I had a star in my hand. As Lisa looked closer at my hand she could see it was the Star of David (I was recalling that the Star of David was a symbol for the sacred marriage of the male and female.) Lisa heard Mary say, *"She sees with her hands. + She can pass the Star to others."* Lisa then said. "This is really strange, I see eyeballs on the tip of your fingers." + We decided the message was to encourage my fingers to type. I was trying hard to find the time to write, but not getting much accomplished.

Several days later when speaking with M.L. on the phone, she laughing said, "I am being shown that you have eyeballs on your fingertips." I answered, "Guess what, Lisa recently told me the same thing. Isn't all this amazing?" M.L. also thought the message was an endorsement for my writings and Jesus'

Heavenly Text messages. ("Thanks, God.")

August 8, 2002. I was awakened as Erv left around 6am. Strangely, I could see myself lying in bed and realized I was out of my body. I was thrilled and tried to walk about my house in spirit form. I've read about out of body experiences so I tried to remain calm and enjoy what was in store. As I continued to lie in bed, I saw and felt very wobbly as my spirit went down the hall into the kitchen. I was having a hard time focusing. When I reached the kitchen, I could only see the hardwood floors. I couldn't seem to get my eyes to focus upward. Then the event abruptly ended and I was back in my bed thanking God. The unusual occurrence had only lasted a short time, but I was grateful to remember the experience. I wondered if I would be doing this often.

September 3, 2002. While trimming flowers in my yard I took a nasty fall. I was standing sideways on a hill removing some dead flowers. I quickly raised up and vigorously pitched them with my left hand to the woods on the other side of the driveway. In doing so, I lost my balance and down I went. I remember thinking that it felt like someone pushed me. I heard a series of crackle, crackle, crackle, as I fell and knew I'd seriously injured myself. I called to Erv who was in the garage. I was experiencing terrible pain in my ankles and we struggled to get me inside. Silently I was calling upon Jesus, Mary, Angels, and MAP (Medical Assistance Program) to please be with me. Erv asked if he should call Dottie and Lisa. I asked hi to put his hands on my ankles. As I lay on the floor in my bedroom I suddenly experienced an excruciating pain in my ankles and my body quivered with pain. Then the pain eased. I asked Erv to get me ice and ibuprofen. Erv wanted to

Heavenly Text

rush me off to the doctor, but I refused. I knew I couldn't get up on my feet to go and: Secondly and most importantly, I felt Spirit had just **set** and **adjusted** my ankles and the Spirit world was watching over me.

Without the use of my feet, I couldn't get into bed so Erv put the mattress on the floor so I could roll in and out. I could then crawl on my knees to the bathroom. Lifting my self up with my arms to go to the bathroom was really hard work and my arms quickly became very sore. I knew I had a challenge ahead of me for some time.

The next morning I called my friends for assistance. I called Anne and she was out, so I left a message. Dottie came rushing over to lay hands on. While working on me she said, "This looks really bad. Call Lisa and have her join us." I immediately phoned Lisa and asked her to come over. She said she couldn't until the afternoon but she immediately looked inside my foot via long distance. Dottie and I both could clearly hear her laughing over the phone. She said, "I'm sorry but this is so funny. I see Jesus taking you by your heels and laying you down, which tells me this is a very spiritual encounter you are having. + When this is over, something wonderful is going to happen. I'm not being shown what that will be, but I think this is connected to someone out of town. When you see that person you will understand." Lisa went on to say, "There is a very bad tear at your right ankle, almost all the way around the bone. You also have a cracked metatarsal bone in your right foot. There's lots of bruising and trauma in there. Your left ankle has a bad sprain on the left side. I imagine you will be laid up for quite some time. It'll probably take four months to totally heal." Dottie was shaking her head and saying, "That's exactly what I am seeing."

The three of us decided that the symbolism of Jesus being

Heavenly Text

in charge of my accident was a strong message that He wanted me "to stop and be still." I presumed it was so I could write and finish the project I wasn't getting around to. I'd certainly have time now. I wondered, "Is this the silence M.L. told me years ago (1997) that I would be called to?"

I also remembered my friend Paola who had started walking the El Camino in Spain the day before. Was that a connection? Had I created this by saying you can walk it for both of us? Was I mirroring her? If so, this was definitely going to be a long healing in distance and in time.

Later that day I called M.L. and told her I'd taken a fall and could she look inside my foot. She said, "This ankle doesn't look good. You know how a T-bone steak looks after the meat is pulled away, like shredded meat still on the bone? Well, that's how your ankle looks." I said, "That's a pretty graphic description. I received the same bad news from my friends here. Anything else?" "Yes, this experience is all very spiritual. I think it has something to do with your writings." (Confirmation.) M.L. continued, "I am now seeing something very interesting. + I see a circle of what appears to be water with a rainbow swirling around in it. (I thought chakras.) Now I see a white dove with a branch in its mouth - the peace sign. Then a little blue bird comes and lands on the branch. + The blue bird has a quill in its mouth and is dipping it back and forth into the water. I am hearing, 'The quill will quench the fire'."

Later when I looked up quench in the dictionary it said - to satisfy. So I presumed I was being told that my writings would satisfy God – "the consuming fire." (Deut. 9-10) ("Thanks, God. A powerful message. I thought of the vision of the trees just months before.)

Erv kept wanting me to go to the doctor but, I refused.

Heavenly Text

"Why?" I insisted, "The trip would be wasting the doctor's and my time because I am not going to let anyone cast my ankle or put a pin in it. I want only Spirit/energy work and I feel foreign objects will only interfere with the energy circulation. I think I'll heal faster this way. I know God is watching over me. I trust my three friends' X-ray vision. I'll be fine."

As friends called to inquire about me I kept hearing, "You can't walk and you are not going to the doctor. What is wrong with you?" (As though I was crazy.) I assured all that I was in good hands and told them about my friends' X-ray vision. I could always feel the doubt in the silence on the other end of the phone. But deep inside I knew God wanted me to be a witness and demonstrate my beliefs in His healing power in what I know to be true.

September 9, 2002. Anne called. "How are you doing? I didn't call sooner because I was out of town" I asked her to look inside my ankles and feet. She responded, "I did the minute I got the message. It looks bad, but I can tell God is very involved with this accident. It appears you are being balanced in more ways than one. Are you able to get up on your feet yet?" "I'm just beginning to be able to with lots of effort," I answered. "I want to get to the computer to write." She said, "It looks to me like you'll have plenty of writing time. I think it will take about two months for you to be able to walk and get about, but about four to six months before it is totally healed. Take care of yourself and you're going to be fine." She described what she was seeing and it matched exactly what the others had told me. "You are being a wonderful witness right now," she said. "Also, do you know someone walking the El Camino? I'm being told this has something to do with that person." "I sure do, and I've already wondered about that," I

Heavenly Text

replied. "The bottom of my feet are even peeling which has nothing to do with sprained ankles. I bet she has blisters." "I'm sure you will eventually understand all," Anne said "Keep up the good work and know you are being used in a powerful way. Smell the flowers along the way."

September 11, 2002. Deanna called saying, "Well, like mother like daughter, I sprained my ankle today while jogging -my right one." I thought, "What are the chances of that?" We discussed her bad accident with her ankle, now nearly twenty years ago. I wondered to myself, "Am I balancing her ankles, too? Or is she helping to balance mine? We truly are one! "

September 13, 2002. I had a dream of riding in a car over a very rough road full of huge planks and rocks. Finally the car came out on a smooth road and I was very relieved. Then the car turned around abruptly and returned to the rough road. I could see grass along the side of the road and remarked, "They need to plant red flowers over there to make this scenery better." I heard, + *"Time to review tough times."* Then I again heard Anne's words. +"Smell the flowers along the way." I smiled inside.

This dream seemed to fit perfectly. Red is the symbol for the root chakra and represents grounding. This right foot experience was constantly reminding me of my left foot experiences ten years ago. Was I being brought into a greater balance of my left and right, yin and yang? Didn't God use my foot ten years ago to prompt me to write? Didn't this dream say review? I seemed to be completing a circle. The dream seem to be an affirmation of where I have been and what I was now going through. Is this the spiraling out like a Labyrinth - the message I received earlier? ("Thanks, God. I'm trying to

Heavenly Text

understand the bigger picture and piece all of the pieces of the puzzle together.")

September 14, 2002. I had a very interesting dream. In my dream, I looked down at my left hand and I couldn't see the jewelry I always wear. My wedding rings and the bracelet that my dad had given me were gone. I felt a deep sense of loss. Then I heard, +*"Look at your right hand."* I did and there was my jewelry on my right hand. I heard, + *"You are just crossing over."*

I prayed, "Thanks, God, I feel this message is an affirmation letting me know my right side and left side are definitely being brought into even a greater balance. Am I going to learn to cross into other realms?

I realize today is the birth date of my daughter Pam and that all of my faith-filled experiences began with her.

I think often about all of the connections of this recent accident, and its deeper meanings. I think of Deanna and her ankle accidents, long ago and recently. I think of Paola on the El Camino and wonder how she is doing. I think of the newly published book, *Healing as a Sacred Path*, written by Robert Keck that I am presently enjoying reading. Keck is describing exactly what I am going through-accepting all that happens to us as healing lessons in life.

As I think back I feel I was told ahead of time, through my dream and visions what was soon to transpire. You knew I needed to stop again, to slow down, to write.

I thank You for all my friends coming daily to administer Spirit/energy work. I know my body is healing quickly. Thanks once again for steering me in the right direction."

Slowly my ankles and feet began to look and feel better.

Heavenly Text

Gradually I was able to withstand some pressure on them and I began to use a walker. It was slow at first, but thank goodness, I was finally able to walk to my computer. With my foot propped up I spent hours typing and condensing my notes. Time seemed to fly by. I was accomplishing what I knew I was supposed to do. Jesus had nudged me once again to fulfill my destiny.

(It was months later that I heard from Paola, and she informed me she had indeed had many blisters walking the Camino, and that she had badly sprained her right ankle. I realized with this experience that God wanted me to understand that distance was no barrier in mirroring healings. Paola and I had helped each other. Were we sisters in another lifetime as she earlier had shared? I don't know for sure. Sisters in this lifetime I know for sure - sisters of the heart. "Thanks, God for enlightening me once again, reminding me how we are all one.")

October 30, 2002. Slowly God is nudging my family. Butch, my older brother, was visiting and surprised me by asking me to show him what I did in my healing work. I was thrilled to administer Spirit/energy work on him. The fact that he didn't elaborate or comment much afterwards didn't bother me. Just the fact that he asked made my heart leap with joy knowing he was trying to understand.

Recently, my son Joe had let me work on his back several times because he had injured it playing basketball. There was no way to measure if Joe got better because of it or if he would have improved on his own. This unknowing is what makes the process so difficult for many to understand. There is not a way to prove anything. (But I knew - from within.)

Grandson Alex feels the energy explicitly and is a joy to

Heavenly Text

share Spirit/energy work with. Once, some time ago, I worked on him when he had streap throat (he was 5 years old). During the process he proceeded to voluntarily announce the colors of the chakras. (Now, how did he know that?) When I was at his throat chakra he said, "Grandma, this is really weird. I see an upside down blue screw." I knew he was seeing the closed throat chakra that was causing his problems. (Only from the mouth of a child would such a statement come.) I continued sharing energy and he suddenly said, "Oops! it's all OK now, it looks like the rest." Days later when I asked him how he was feeling he said, "Oh, I went in and checked and everything is OK."

As I've written before, the new minds are entering and change is on the horizon. I know God is paving the way for understanding among those I love. I have been waiting patiently.

October 31, 2002. Around midnight I woke up. I began to see a vision of a large document. + I was trying to read it when the letters on the page all started to fall off. I watched them all slide to the bottom and rapidly enter a funnel. Instantly I felt a pressure in my chest and felt the letters had gone inside of me. I then saw in a vision the written words, **His Word is within you.** +

What a gift. I was overcome with joy. I repeatedly thanked God for the message and felt this was an affirmation that my condensing my writings was exactly what He wanted. An affirmation that His Word is within us all, we just have to believe and find it.

November 1, 2002. My friend Colette and I went to Kansas City to attend a conference, "Living in the Mind of

Heavenly Text
God," given by Gregg Braden. Braden is the author of many books, (*Awakening to Zero Point, Walking Between Two Worlds, Isaiah Effect, Lost Mode of Prayer, The Divine Matrix, The God Code*. All have been a great source of inspiration to me. Back in the 90's when I was wrestling with so many thoughts, I found his scientific approach very comforting. Braden has had careers in the earth sciences and aerospace industries and is excellent at sharing his wisdom. He considers himself a bridge between science and spirituality. All of his work seems to affirm and add depth to the topics I've written about.

I took many notes during the workshop. Braden refers to the time we are living in as the Shift of Ages--a time of unprecedented changes and the close of a great super cycle. In the workshop Braden explained what previous ages of civilization have gone through, over millions of years, each time there has been a shift. He says these shifts have happened at least fourteen times. He writes, "The relationship between the earth, the planetary magnetic fields, and cellular function of the body are key components to the understanding of conscious evolution and the process of the shift." (I have always felt his explanations correlate with the cataclysmic messages from Mother Mary.) He writes, "To the degree you are able to love without fear, experience without judgment and allow through compassion, to that degree are you preparing yourself to survive the Shift emotionally and psychologically, as well as physically."

He explains how the earth's magnetic field is dropping and its vibrations are increasing. "The earth is changing physical dynamics. From the perspective of earth science, the changing paradigm is accomplished through a realignment of two digital, measurable, fundamental parameters: those of planetary

Heavenly Text

frequency and planetary magnetics. These parameters alone have a far-reaching and profound impact upon human consciousness, human thought, and the behavior of matter in general."

His in-depth research of ancient literature adds validity to his words and work. His research on the effects of prayer, especially prayer of gratitude and appreciation, were extremely interesting. After his remarks and the groups' participation in various demonstrations, I decided I was definitely supposed to leave all of my "Thanks, God" quotes in my writings. Braden explained, "Heart based feelings and emotions change the chemistry of our bodies and produce pockets of energy that can change our physical world." In essence Braden teaches that we all have the power to affect the prevailing energy of ourselves and of our world. (Possibly my witnessing to this will help others.)

Braden explained how a growing body of evidence suggests that focusing our feelings of appreciation and gratitude, as if a prayer has already been answered has a measurable effect on the quality of prayer. This kind of prayer has no words, no outward expression, but is based on feelings. Rather than praying for someone to 'win' 'loose', 'suffer' or 'heal', we have the opportunity to 'feel' the appreciation and gratitude for the peace and healing that already exists. The power of this kind of prayer transcends winners and losers — inviting us to elevate the conditions of our world to a new realm beyond win/loss. In doing so, we open the door of a very subtle, yet powerful principle that allows for the possibility of peace/healing to be present without imposing our will to make it so."

In other words, our prayers need to originate from our

Heavenly Text
heart, not our head. I believe this is what I do in my Spirit/energy work and balance is created.

A true gift from the Braden workshop was the availability of ancient writings, such as The *Dead Sea Schrolls*, *The NagHammadi Library*, *Essene Writing*s, and books by historians. I had wanted to learn more about the Essenes ever since Lisa told me we once lived in their community. In my research I discovered the word Essene has been traced back to a Aramaic word, "assaya", which means doctor or healer. Coins have helped establish the chronology of the Essenes to be as early as the 4th Century B.C. In various texts the Essenes refer to themselves as the New Covenant, the Holy Community, the Poor Ones, Sons of Light, God's Chosen and Men of Truth. Their lifestyle was one of sharing everything. All goods and money were common property. Some were celibate, some were married. Their way of life enabled them to live to advanced ages of 120 years or more, and they were said to have marvelous strength and endurance. In all of their activities they expressed creative love. It appears they were the true precursors of Christianity. They sent out healers and teachers into the world from their brotherhood, amongst them were Elijah, John the Baptist, John the Beloved, and the great Essene Master, Jesus.

The Essenes taught that we all have a power that lives within us, a web of energy that links us all together, and the power of human emotion links all of creation together. They seemed to understand the wisdom of the heavens, the history of the world, the secrets of our origin, how our relationships work with one another, how to heal our bodies, and how to heal the cosmos. It is very clear that the Essenes believed in the immortal life of the soul, Spirit survives its body. The Essenes

Heavenly Text

say we came to this world by choice to find love and to establish love here on earth. They wrote that it is through love and compassion that we evolve into Sons and Daughters of Light. Some of the Essenes wrote the Dead Sea Scrolls, which are now known to contain duplicates of the Essene Gospels.

What I understand about the history of the Dead Sea Scrolls is a council was called by Emporer Constantine, to gather and assemble information from ancient writings. At that time, the Council removed twenty five complete books from the Biblical text and put twenty more aside for just the educated to read. Then, in 1946, when the Dead Sea Scrolls were found, scholars discovered text that had not been seen for over 2000 years. The Scrolls were found by a young Bedouin shepherd boy. He found them in a cave near the Dead Sea, while searching for a lost sheep. In the cave he found clay vessels that contained ancient Scrolls. Later, numerous more were found at Qumran. Since then, these texts are painstakingly being transcribed and slowly being released to the public. These ancient writings help clarify many misconceptions that have been passed down in the name of religion. They prove to me that there needs to be a major re-evaluation of early Christian history.

I especially enjoyed reading a series of books I bought at Braden's workshop, *The Essene Gospel of Peace* by Edmund Bordeaux Szekely. He is the author of over 80 books published in many countries on philosophy and ancient cultures. He spoke eight languages and during the years 1927-1947. Bordeauz wrote and published many books on the Essenes based on historical sources such as the works of Joseph Flavis, Philo, and Plinis, and on manuscripts in the archives of the Library of the Vatican, the Library of the Habsburg in Vienna,

Heavenly Text

and the Library of the British Museum. He also helped translate the Dead Sea Scrolls. It was in 1927 that Bordeaux published his first translation of the ancient manuscript he found in the Secret Archives of the Vatican. Bordeaux also later helped translate some of the Dead Sea Scrolls and discovered many duplicates that he had previously translated from the Vatican.

The Gospel of Peace is an accumulation of messages from Jesus on how to become Sons of Light. These writings explain the importance of our connection with God's Angels and the mysteries of the Law. The Law is considered the living word of God to prophets for living man. Also it explains the importance of our connection with All and how our thoughts create our reality.

Chills abounded as I read, "When the flower opens from the bud the angels of sun and water bring it to its time of blossoming," + (I recalled my vision of long ago, a flower coming up out of the ground, when I first met Anne) And, "...the unknown angels of the Heavenly Father taught them through their sleeping hours." + (I've certainly experienced that.)

I'll list here also a few of Jesus' quotes from these writings that deeply resonated with me:

"Behold the Tree of Life growing eternal branches to sink its branches into an eternal source..." (My tree dreams.)

"I tell you truly your body was made not only to breathe, and eat, and think, but it was also made to enter the Holy Stream of Life. (The power of Spirit/energy that I feel.)

"And your ears were made to hear the sound of the Father." (My +'s.)

"Around and around you have come on your journey. You have made of your body a holy temple wherein dwell the

Heavenly Text
angels of God. Many years have you shared the daylight with the angels of Earthly Mother; many years you have slept in the arms of the Heavenly Father, taught by unknown angels. You have learned the laws of the Son of Man are seven, of the angels three, and of God which is One." (Is there a time schedule for being initiated into the ways of God? (7-3-1 ?)

"After seven years of laboring you will be given the gift of tongues so you may draw to you the full power of the Earthly Mother." (I experienced this after my Grand Mal Kudalini.)

"And the day will come when all will enter the Brotherhood of the Elect, and learn the hidden teachings of the Elders, even those of Enoch and before." (Enoch's words revealed to me via the Phoenix years ago.)

"The Heavenly Father hath kindled his flame in the hearts of Children of Light." (Lisa seeing the flame at my heart and recently seeing a flame over my head.)

"I tell you truly all that is green and with life has the power of the angel of the Sun." (My green mist dream? Anjail seeing the green?)

"The Law is the living word of the living God to living prophets for living man." (My vision of October 31, 2002.)

"Peace be with you," was written in the Essene Gospel over and over as words of encouragement for the Essenes and I'm sure for all of mankind, especially for me at this time. All of this information certainly brought me peace. Also Jesus explained reincarnation in these writings by explaining how a blade of grass starts as a seed, grows, withers and goes back into the ground only to be born again, the same as it is with man. Jesus said, "For life always begins again."

I pray, "Jesus I am overwhelmed with feelings of joy and understanding. Thanks for the information, confirmation,

Heavenly Text
and affirmations You continue to send my way. Continue to teach me more and more. You and Your angels have definitely taught me in my waking hours and hours of sleep. Although I don't understand all, You are filling me with Your peace and joy. I know **I Am** being used as Your messenger for a larger audience as **I AM** being initiated into Your Brotherhood. Thanks be to God.

I can't help but think of the screech owl that was here seven days, gone three days, and back one day. Was the time line of man's initiation the message the owl was conveying to me - to let me know I am progressing in Your ways? I reviewed my past and realize it was exactly seven years from my first night of seeing the Light, May 1993, to my Grand Mal Kudalini experience of March 2000 when I spoke in tongues and knew I was totally connected to You. And it was seven years from Christmas of 1994 when You showed me Your exposed Sacred Heart to December 2001 when I had the vision video of the pyramid and eye. I wonder which seven years You go by. My heart jumps for joy in anticipation for what the future holds. Thanks be to God."

It's very interesting to me that we do not hear more about the important information contained in these or other ancient writings from the pulpit of religious leaders. It has been a monumental task for many transcribing the scrolls and other ancient writings over the last fifty years, but I know in God's time all will be revealed.

I also find similarities between Hinduism and Christian traditions very evident in the Scroll writings that I've read. In ancient times not many individuals understood or could read Sanskrit, so I believe the connection was not made between these two sects until the Scrolls were found. Jesus (an Essene)

Heavenly Text

taught brotherly love, self respect, good deeds, and shared with the poor, very similar to the Buddhist teachings. Since we read nothing in the scriptures about Jesus from age 12 to 30, is it possible Jesus was educated not only by the Essenes but also in India? Many seem to think so. Did Jesus speak in parables because He did not wish to propagate a new religion? It fascinates me that the Essenes are not even mentioned in the New Testament and they were very prevalent at that time. Was it because there are obvious parallels between the Essenes and Buddhist monasteries? Did the Church intentionally remove this evidence? Did the Church decide to make Jesus what they wanted Him to be?

December 24, 2002. My friend Bill, who has lived in the nursing home for the last ten years, died on this Christmas Eve. What a marvelous Christmas gift for him. I'm confident he is rejoicing at being out of his crippled, paralyzed body. He just went to sleep and did not wake up. I was told by the doctor that he had pneumonia, unknown to anyone, and carbon monoxide had built up in his body. What a beautiful, peaceful way God took him home. There was no way for Bill to know how much he taught me by his patient acceptance of his condition. (But then, I know that he does now know.)

I pray, "Thanks, God, for bringing him into my life. And many thanks for taking him out of my life in such a beautiful peaceful way. I'm so happy he is finally at home."

December 30, 2002. I was administering Spirit/energy work on someone when the person began to see. Her spiritual eye was opened. In her mind's eye, she began to see. She said she was above and could see me working on her. I told her to look inside her body, and she was able to. I guided her, as I've

Heavenly Text

done others, how to look at her organs, check her blood, check her bones, etc. (I have taught dozens Spirit/energy work, and several have developed this second sight. My students have been men and women from different religious backgrounds. All have deep faith - faith in the unknown - and they in turn have gone out and helped others. The circle grows larger each year.)

Deep inside, I was jealous that another person was given spiritual sight for their healing work. Why not me? Then I heard very clearly, + *"Nancy, Don't you get it? If you had spiritual sight when working on others, all might think you create your visions on your own. This way, all will know the visions are from the heavens. From Me. Having others to speak from the heavens to you gives more credence to your writings. All will know that I work with You on another level."*

I began to shed tears and thanked Jesus for the message that made complete sense to me.

January 1, 2003. Another year begins. I write here a few words that express my thoughts for this past year.

Christianity has been my path. I know Catholicism is the religion I needed in this lifetime to find Christ within. I believe, though, that anyone can find the way, the truth, and the life in many and varying circumstances, religions, and cultures. I have found that by not letting theology or the status quo of society restrict me, my life has become a wonderful adventure. The bottom line is that awakening Spiritual energy is something unique between each of us and the Spirit within us. Mankind and the world is vast and we are evolving on many levels. Life is a process of experiencing multidimensional worlds. It is imperative that mankind realizes that the Divine Word of God did not stop with Jesus, the apostles, and ancient

Heavenly Text

prophets, but continues today.

God revealed Himself through Christ to teach mankind what humanity was "to be" and "to show" us the way. Since Christ's time on earth, it appears to me that mankind has worshipped the external symbols and outward ceremonies instead of finding Spirit within. Mankind has equated religion with faith, instead of love of God and neighbor. True Spiritual evolution is all about being seized by God, in the self quest for knowledge and understanding of His ways, to become one with Him by living in love with all.

We all need to learn to honor life and instill love in all we do: in how we think; in how we share; in how we react; in how we support each other; and in how we support our planet. It all boils down to kindness, compassion, and non-violence. What we do for others comes back to us. I believe in the quote, "We will know them by their fruits." (Matt 7:20)

"Thanks be to God."

Even though I do not adhere to all of the beliefs and teachings of my religion, I still go to Mass often (four or five times a week), to give Jesus the praise He deserves. I believe my presence, worshipping with a community, shows of my deep love for Christ. I am committed to hanging in there, through thick or thin, through chaos, misunderstandings, opposition and condemnation, to demonstrate by my faith what I know to be true.

We read in the Bible that Enoch, Elijah, Moses, and Jesus ascended. I now believe many more have done the same. I'm convinced I can, too. Jesus came to show us the way. I now look forward to the further evolution of my soul and ascending into other dimensions.

***

Heavenly Text

June 8, 2003. I just finished spending four days at "Cedars of Peace," (retreat cabins in the woods at Loretto) where my mother now lives. She had a stroke in January 2003 and needed skilled nursing care. We moved her to the Loretto Motherhouse in Nerinx, Kentucky. The family feels at peace knowing her care there is exceptional.

I walked the half mile daily to visit Mom. Again, Mom told me about "living in two worlds." When I pressed her for more information she said, "I don't know how to explain. It scares me. It's so different. I am fearful because it is something I don't understand." When Mom and I went to Mass and heard the Gospel of John "They do not belong to the world any more than I belong to the world...." I said to her, "See, Jesus knew it was different in the heavenly realm. You won't die but just go to another dimension." She smiled and seemed to accept. I told her to not be afraid, that God was preparing her by teaching her little by little, that death was simply a transition into another state and nothing to fear.

I took this manuscript to read, to reflect on. Then Spirit seemed to come into play. Each morning at my cabin, I was awakened by a male Cardinal bird tapping on the glass of the picture window that looked out into the beautiful scenery of the woods and nature. The Cardinal did not use a gentle tap, but many times hammered away until I would get out of bed and go to the window. Then the bird would fly away. I began to take serious notice when this happened on the second morning, and it continued all four mornings. Was this another + via a bird?

When I looked up Cardinal in *Animal Speak* it said, "A Cardinal bird's presence reflects a time to renew our vitality. It reflects lessons in developing and accepting a new sense of our own true self-importance." Was Spirit telling me through this

Heavenly Text

bird "to get up and get moving?" Was this about my writings? Let your book fly out to the world? I remembered the previous experiences with Jesus and the color red, and wondered if He was again asking to get deeper into my heart, by releasing His writings.

When journaling I asked Jesus these questions and I heard. +*"My child, you are my servant. Be patient. Yes, I'll help you. Go forth with your writings. I need you to help My people. Tell My people more and more. My words are within you. Go forth with My messages. The world needs to know."*

I asked, "When?" "Where?"

I heard, +*"Sit in stillness each day and ask for My Spirit and My Power to fill you. Not just when working with other's but for yourself. Ask more for yourself and let My Spirit fill you, just you, over and over."*

At the cabin when meditating while gazing out my window at a huge Cedar tree (sixty feet tall or taller), I heard + *"You are like this tree."* I couldn't help but remember my many tree dreams. I especially remembered a dream of many years ago in which I was decorating a huge Cedar tree for Christmas when I suddenly saw a "White Spirit" inside of it. I promptly said to the Spirit, "You don't want to stay in there. I leave my tree up for a good month or more and you won't be able to sit down." I tried to lift the tree off the "White Spirit" by pulling the tree over its head. I woke up. I wondered then about the dream's deeper meaning. I now believe this was when Spirit was prompting me, trying to get my attention, to find my Spirit within. That dream was before I began to write, before my foot problems. I've had many tree dreams since then. It's been a long fruitful journey. I also recalled my recent Cedar tree dream, decorated with animals, and remembered a Cardinal had been in that tree.

Heavenly Text

I realize I have become like a tree. My branches have grown, my roots are planted in the earth, and my eyes are reaching to the heavens. I have finally found my higher self, the Spirit within.

I know birds are messengers from heaven. Back in March I had a dream in which I asked Spirit where I was on the ladder of my spirituality. I saw written on a document "11" (again the total of 7-3-1). + I was pleased then and now I believe I have reached another phase. I know the Cardinal bird's visit was conveying all of this to me, and that I'm on my way to the next level. I wonder how many levels there are. Time will tell.

I guess one can say I walked away from Cedars of Peace with "peace in my heart" knowing that I always write the truth and I am finally free. Free to speak my peace - free to venture out with the Word of God.

Since writing this section I have a renewed and stronger sense of knowing, courage, and understanding. I am ready to release Jesus' messages to the world. (Thanks, God.)

More Gifts

Since I have reached a deeper peace and comfort, it is easier to voice my feelings and intentions about my calling. I am able to speak without wondering what others think. I know what I know, and that is all there is to it. But I haven't heard from Spirit where to go with my writings. I wait patiently.

August 15, 2003. God sent me a vision that brought hope for the future. + A huge bright circle of Light opened up in my mind's eye and I could see, in the left side of the circle, men milling around. They seemed to have something black over their faces. They had unusual hats on. I realized one was a Swiss guard, and that I must be seeing something in the Vatican. Then a man's face began to appear in the center of the brightness, which took up about two-thirds of the circle. I did not know who he was. He was older and had a small round face, touch of gray hair, and wore glasses. Over his right shoulder I saw the Pope sitting in a highback chair, with his head slumped over (like we often see Pope John Paul II). I couldn't imagine what the images were telling me. Then I heard, + *"He knows what you know. He will speak out in time."*

Was I possibly seeing the future pope or a cardinal who would in time clear up all the misunderstandings and dispel all

Heavenly Text

of the secrets within Christianity? I believe the other men milling around were possibly cardinals, and Spirit was letting me know they are in the dark. They are acting in good faith. They just don't know.

I had an immediate sense of peace and contentment, knowing that I was not alone in the information I was writing. Someone is going to help. I know I will recognize this person if I ever see the face again.

I prayed, "Thanks, God. What wonderful news! I'm so thrilled to be part of this bigger picture. I wonder when? Is this when my writings will be needed?"

August 23, 2003. I had a prophetic dream. + I saw and witnessed a man jumping into water. He was not dressed. Then the strangest thing. I saw his penis begin to grow, longer and longer (I had thoughts of Pinnochio). In time the penis grew long enough that the man put his own penis in his mouth. Then his legs and feet dropped off, and it looked more like a snake holding its tail in its mouth.

When I woke I thought it a strange dream, yet I thought I remembered a symbol depicting this. Later, I came across the picture of this symbol: Ouroboros, a gnostic term that means great white serpent, an alchemy symbol for completion and wholeness. In Egyptian symbolism, the snake represents the body. So, was Spirit letting me know I had reached a completion? Possibly a completion of totally balancing my male side.

September 20, 2003. I had a dream that a person carrying a baby came to visit. As the baby was placed in a chair I realized the baby was only a "head." I remember thinking, "How can that be?" The person said, *"The baby is going to be*

Heavenly Text

fine." + I asked the nature of this handicap and was amazed someone could live without a body.

When I woke I wondered if Spirit was telling me we don't need our bodies? Or am I too much in my head? Needless to say I analyze, and question all of the time. Was it a symbol for me? I know I give from my heart but I often function from my head. I'm constantly trying to think my way out of things, always double-guessing and questioning.

December 24, 2003. I began to see a lot of Light. As the Light moved and rotated, it took on the shape of a train engine. I heard, + *"You are now the engine."* Was I being told I was going forward again? I remembered the train dream of May 13, 2000. In that dream, I was standing in a train engine with the engineer when a tiny baby was brought, and I was told I would be the guardian of the baby. I remember hearing at that time *"Going Forward."* Was I the baby and now I'm grown and the engine? Have I reached completion as indicated by my earlier dream?

January 10, 2004. While lying in bed with my eyes closed, I began to see lots of activity in my mind's eye. I was awake. The Lights were fast and I couldn't make out what I was seeing. Then I would hear, + *"Open your eyes."* and I would open my eyes and see nothing. I would close my eyes and see objects again that I couldn't totally distinquish. Then I would see a book with pictures of the body. Again I heard, + *"Open your eyes."* but when I did I saw nothing. This procedure repeated several times. Did they mean my spiritual eyes? (I gave thanks as the process ended and said, "I'm trying to figure out how to do this God. Help me.")

Heavenly Text

February 22, 2004. An awareness during the night. + I saw a thin, gauzy, shadowy, filmy substance removed from my feet. This repeated several times until it appeared that it was down to the bone where I saw redness and rawness.

I wondered what in the world this was about? Thoughts of stigmata came to me.

April 7, 2004. As I walked into my room where I see individuals for Spirit/energy work I saw a card lying upset down in the middle of the room on the floor. I picked it up and turned it over. It was a picture of St. Francis of Assisi. I wondered how it had gotten there. I had been in the room the evening before and it had not been there. I felt perplexed yet thankful, as it seemed a gift brought by an angel. + But why? Very interesting.

April 13, 2004. Anne was passing through and came for a short visit. It was great seeing her since it had been two and a half years since she had been to Columbia. When we were doing Spirit/energy work she remained at my feet for a long, long time. I asked what was going on and she said she was seeing a stigmata as Spirit guided her hands. Anne remarked that possibly I had a stigmata in a previous life and the cellular memory was now releasing. We discussed at length how our bodies have cellular memory from this life and other lifetimes. I know from my Spirit/energy work that former body imprints need to be deprogrammed. I told Anne about my dream of seeing something removed from my feet. I reminded her of our two-way dream many years ago, when I called her and she had heard the words stigmata. I also began to recall the many times stigmata has come up in my dreams and visions, and how M.L. had said she felt I had an "invisible stigmata." I remembered

Heavenly Text

how the doctor had remarked he had never seen a growth like the one I had. We discussed the fact that I found the picture of St. Francis, but that it did not necessarily mean I was St. Francis in another lifetime; that it could be Spirit's way of getting the message across. After all, we are all one in Spirit.

I was prompted to read more on past lives and generational healing. I find the subject fascinating, although there is no way to prove anything. I just thanked God for the final release, knowing this transformation had taken ten years. I believe this was the completion that my dream of the Ouroborus was conveying to me.

May 13, 2004. I found my glasses. I must explain. About six weeks earlier I had lost my new prescription eyeglasses. They seemed to have just disappeared. I remembered reading with them one afternoon, and the next morning I simply could not find them. I looked and looked. Other than being at home, I had only been to the grocery store. I went there and went through their lost and found with no luck. I wore my old glasses and kept hoping the glasses would show up I kept asking my angels to please find them. I finally gave up after a couple of weeks and purchased another pair.

Then on this special day of the 13th, I was at my kitchen sink preparing dinner. I was using the disposal when it suddenly stopped. I looked under the sink to try to fix it. Shocked, I found my glasses lying in the dark under the disposal! I laughed out loud declaring, "Thank you angels for finding my glasses. What a funny place to hide them. What kind of message is this?"

I know there was no way I had put them there. What a funny feeling wondering how this happened. I thought and

Heavenly Text

thought. I wondered if the angels were telling me, "We have been keeping you in the dark." Or "We didn't want you to change your prescription, we are working on your eyes as they are." Or "You won't be needing these much longer." Who knows?

When Erv got home I asked him to please fix the disposal and told him I had found my glasses there. He looked at me as if I had lost it. Laughing I said, "Did you put them there? I know I sure didn't." I still can't help but wonder!

May 22, 2004. Lisa C. was at my home. We shared Spirit/energy work. I told her about finding the glasses under the sink. She laughed saying, "As you were telling me the story, I could see little angels laughing and laughing as they put them there." (Affirmation? I think so.) We both laughed thinking how funny Spirit can be to get a point across. We decided they must definitely be working with my eyes. Am I going to get spiritual sight when working on others?

I also shared with Lisa that I been feeling a lot of heart symptoms and didn't know if it was me. She checked my heart and said I was fine. She then checked Erv's heart (at a distance) and discovered a blockage in an artery in the back of his heart. This scared us. I didn't think Erv would believe me. I decided this was serious and I didn't care what Erv thought, I had to tell him. I had to get him to a doctor. When I told Erv he acted as if it was all nonsense, but I insisted and insisted that we needed to check this information out. If Lisa was wrong, he could laugh at us. If she was right he would be glad he did. He finally agreed to an appointment with a heart doctor.

June 1, 2004. In a dream, I was driving down a narrow road. As I rounded a curve, I could see lots of big rocks and

Heavenly Text

boulders in the road. I knew it was going to be a bumpy ride, if possible to navigate at all. I looked back through the car's rear window to see if I could turn the car around. I heard very clearly, +*"Don't look back, go forward, not much further."*

When I woke up, I thought of Erv and his heart and wondered if there would be rocky times ahead and perhaps this was Spirit's way of letting me know. More lessons to learn! I recalled my earlier dream of the rocky road, when I sprained my ankles and broke my foot in 2002.

June 15, 2004. Erv and I went to see the heart doctor. In the waiting room, when Erv was filling out papers there was a question, "Who referred you?" I chuckled inside when I saw Erv write down "wife." When we got into the examing room the doctor walked in and looked directly at me and asked, "What is this wife referral?' I asked him if he had ever heard of a medical intuitive. He said, "No." I explained that I know severa,l and they can see inside of the body. I explained that a friend of mine was a medical intuitive, and she saw a blocked artery in the back of Erv's heart. The doctor tried to not smirk and said, "I'm sure you are fine Erv, but we will check you out anyway." After the initial exam the doctor said Erv was fine, but he would order an echogram before and after a stress test to satisfy me.

As I expected, the tests showed Erv did have a problem in the back of his heart. The doctor said he wanted to do a heart catherization for further diagnosis. The doctor explained he was leaving on vacation the next morning and would be gone a week. He scheduled Erv to be first on the list when he returned on the 22nd.

June 16, 2004. At my request, my son Joe went to see the

Heavenly Text

eye doctor. I have been after him for a couple of years to go get checked for glaucoma, since Erv has glaucoma and it is definitely hereditary. [Erv's grandmother went blind because she didn't discover she had glaucoma until it was too late.] At Easter, Joe had told me he had finally made an appointment at the insistence of me and his wife, and because he thought he may need reading glasses. When the eye doctor looked into Joe's eyes, he said he saw something he didn't like and sent Joe for an immediate MRI. Joe went directly for the test, but they were closing for the day. They told Joe to come back first thing in the morning. Joe called and told me about the scheduled MRI. I called Lisa C. immediately, but she was out. I left a detailed message.

Joe called the next morning with the shocking information: "Mom, I have a brain tumor." Devastating news to hear. I immediately went to his office and saw the film from the MRI, which showed a huge tumor (the size of an orange) in back of his eyes and nose. The eye doctor had called the neurosurgeon and Joe was to see him later that day. As expected, the neurosurgeon told Joe he needed immediate surgery. The doctor explained there were some further tests that needed to be done before he could operate, and that he was leaving the next day on vacation, but Joe would be first on the lists when he got back on the 29th. He explained to Joe that it was going to be a very long surgery - that it was the biggest meningioma tumor he had ever seen. The doctor was very up front and told Joe everything. He told Joe he had to have had the tumor for a long time. He asked if any of us had noticed any personality changes. (We had, but thought stress had caused the personality changes. Other than that there had been no signs or pain other than occasional headaches Joe had attributed to his allergies). The doctor didn't think the tumor

Heavenly Text

was malignant because it was a meningioma. He explained to Joe that he would not probe into the eye, (if the tumor was attached to the eye) but would leave some of the tumor, which would mean further surgery down the road. He told Joe he could not guarantee that he would not have to go into the brain. All scary news to say the least. I couldn't believe it. In two days time, I learned that both of my men were having serious health problems. (Definitely a rocky road ahead!)

Lisa C. called later that afternoon and said, "I hate to tell you this, but Joe has a serious problem and needs to get to the doctor right away." I told her we had already found out. She said she didn't want to be the one to tell me what she was seeing and was grateful we already knew.

For some reason I didn't come unglued, but knew all was in God's hands. In fact, it felt orchestrated from the heavens with both of them finding out at the same time. With both doctors going on vacation, they would be rested to operate on my loved ones.

It was a terribly long week, with not much sleep for all of us, wondering about the outcomes.

June 22, 2004. I went with Erv for his heart catherization. Afterwards, the doctor came to talk to me and said, "Erv has a 60 to 70% blockage in an artery in the back of his heart. I want to confer with my colleagues, but I don't want to do anything right now with your son's problems and all. We'll just see Erv in a month. You don't have to worry. Erv won't have to have open-heart surgery. When and if we do something, we will put in a stint."

The doctor did not once mention the fact about my knowledge ahead of time, or that he even remembered why we had come to him in the first place. I wanted to say,"I told you

Heavenly Text

so--my friend was right," but I thought best to say nothing. I was glad to not have to think about open heart surgery. ("Thanks, God.")

As you can imagine, Erv started becoming a believer from this experience. His heart was more open to medcal intuitive information and Spirt/energy work. At last! + I prayed a huge, "Thanks, God."

June 23, 2004. The next day Joe's wife had to work, so I took Joe for his brain catherization. The doctor explained the procedure as how it was the same as a heart catherization, but he would go on up into the brain. Joe said, "Yeah, my dad had one of those yesterday." The doctor and nurse both looked shocked and gave their regrets that we were going through this, back to back. What are the odds!

During Joe's procedure, while waiting in the waiting room I put my reading glasses on that normally hang around my neck, and I suddenly realized one of the lenses was gone. I could put my finger through the eye frame. The lens must have fallen out on the way to the hospital. Upset that I had lost it, I had to wait in silence. So, I just shut my eyes, and tried to visualize all was going well with Joe's procedure.

Three hours later, the doctor came out and told me all went as expected, and that the surgeon would be happy with the pictures. I prayed another "Thank you," hoping this meant the tumor wasn't protruding into the eyes or brain.

(Here was another happening with my glasses. Did Spirit use the time to work on my eyes again? I guess so. Later, (in 2010) my eye doctor said I did not need glasses any more - just readers. Thanks, God.)

Heavenly Text

June 24, 2004. Some good news. I got a phone call from Anne that she was passing through town on her way to Kansas City, "Could you meet me for lunch?" I felt God was sending me some comfort and strength. It was great seeing her and we discussed at length all of the ramifications of brain surgery. She told me it appeared to her that Joe had had the tumor for many years. We talked about the correlation between Erv and Joe's problems, and the syncronicity of it all, even the fact that she was here. I shared the stories of my eye glasses, wondering if there was a connection. We discussed the correlation between father-son, the heart-third eye, and on and on. She said, "It feels divinely orchestrated from the heavens." I agreed and said, "I have already thought of that. I doubt if I'll ever understand the ramifications of it all."

June 25, 2004. I received a call that Mom was taken to the emergency room because she kept passing out. My entire family was falling apart! I knew I couldn't go to Kentucky to be with her. I was needed at home. It turned out her problems were from some medication she was taking. Mom is sure strong. She has her ups and downs, but she is still here with us.

June 29, 2004. Joe's surgery lasted nine hours. It consisted of making an incision from ear to ear, rolling back the skin on his forehead, and cutting a large hole in the front of the skull to remove the massive tumor. A long day indeed. I stayed home mediatating, praying, visualizing that the doctor's hands were being guided by Spirit. After the surgery Joe was only in recovery for an hour, and then brought to intensive care where we could visit him. He immediately knew us. He was talking away, excited to be alive. The doctor had originally told him he would be on a respirator for 24 hours and probably

Heavenly Text

not know anyone for hours; so he was elated. He could see and hear. He had his memory with no apparent side effects. I stood at the end of his bed clearing the anesthetic from his body by holding his feet, when he stated firmly, "Mom, I don't know what you are doing, but you are making my feet so hot. Take your hands off." Instead I held my hands about a foot above his feet and continued clearing his body. Shortly, he said, "I can see your hands aren't touching me, but you are making my feet so hot. Please move." I did as I was told, knowing I had accomplished the task.

When they got Joe out of bed the next day for the first time, he had what they called a mild seizure--a blank stare, no shaking. He was taken for a body scan and all appeared fine. The doctor ordered medicine to prevent the possiblility of further seizures. Joe was heavily medicated and began to sleep more. He was moved to a private room within 48 hours. His wife Kathy spent the night in the room with him. I arrived the next morning, to give her a break and she went to breakfast. As Joe slept, I sat beside his bed and began Spirit/energy work. God gave me a gift. + I could SEE (with my eyes open) Joe's spirit lift and hover over his body. Then I could SEE angels working on his head. It brought tears of gratitude and I knew, without a doubt, Joe was going to be fine.

I prayed, "Thanks, God. I never cease to be amazed. You have carried me through these last months. I am forever grateful for understanding how important it is to put my trust in You."

On July 4, 2004. Joe got to come home. His quick recovery was surprising all. He was 42 years old, in good condition, and his body was responding beautifully. I was the designated driver to take him home because of the size of our

Heavenly Text

car. We were standing in the kitchen when it was time for me to depart, when Joe gave me a big hug saying, "Mom thanks for everything." I cannot explain what happened but I felt a surge, a power, a deep interior "hum" went through my body. + (I said nothing but wondered to myself, "What was that all about? Was I clearing or receiving? Was Spirit balancing our energy? Was Joe sharing some of the energy I saw Spirit give him? Was Joe full of a new kind of energy because of his experience? Who knows?") Joe did agree to have me come to work on him throughout the week. I took my table and did more Sprit/energy and CranioSacral on him. I was wondering if I should touch his head or not, but as I brought my hands close to his head, I could feel a strong force stop my hands about ten inches away. I thanked the angels for guiding me. I held my hands in mid-air until a balance was reached. The second time I worked on him, I felt a strong force stop my hands about three inches away from his head, where I remained until I felt balance. The third time I worked on him, my hands gently rested on his head, and I felt a tremendous sense of stillness and quiet take place.

Joe continued to recover and was back at work in three week's time, even though the doctor had originally told him he would be off work for at least six weeks.

I prayed, "Thanks, God. I know when I work on others, I benefit from the energy as much as they do. I remember my dream about the head. Now I am wondering if the dream was showing me that my son was going to have head problems, and all would be fine and I was not to worry? Thanks for guiding my hands. Thanks for keeping me calm. Thanks for Spirit/energy work. I pray soon all will understand and use this power that You so graciously share with us. "

Heavenly Text

July 6, 2004. A meeting at Boone hospital. I presented them with a check for the installation of a labyrinth. My many hours of healing work and collecting funds for this project had finally come to fruition. I was thrilled. It had taken three years of deciding where and when, but the project was finally going to begin.

Recently, I had contacted Robert Ferre (the gentlemen I met after having my dream who is the foremost builder of labyrinths in the U.S.) to see if he would install it for us. He had developed a method of putting the labyrinth pattern into concrete. When I asked him how much he charged, he told me $18,000. The next day when my bank statement came it was "exactly" that amount. I guess the angels were waiting in the wings until I had collected the correct amount of funds.

The hospital signed the contract with Robert, and he was to begin September 23rd. Work quickly began on preparing the spot. The money obtained for this labyrinth had included many, many hours of heart to heart work with many persons. Because of this, I made a small scroll with all the names of those who contributed to this project, placed it in a container, and buried it where the heart of the labyrinth would be. I knew with this gesture that the energy and love of many would be with each person who walked this labyrinth.

August 13, 2004. A gift on Mary's day. At night I had a powerful vision experience. + I saw energy coming from the earth swirling like a tornado. Then I saw energy coming from the heavens swirling like a tornado. The two swirling tornado energies began to merge and were spiraling together. Then they collapsed and they became a labyrinth.

I was thrilled to see this display showing me that the labyrinth is definitely a way to balance of the heavens and

Heavenly Text
earth. I wondered if Spirit was telling me they were balancing the energy where our labyrinth was being put in. I believe so.

On the 12th of September, Robert Ferre called and said he was coming early to start cutting the pattern into the concrete. The concrete had been curing for a month, so we were ready. How appropriate to begin the project on Mary's date of the thirteenth. It was also the date of a new moon.

September 13, 2004. After Robert and his two helpers had marked out the pattern and were about to begin, they noticed a praying mantis had found its way to the exact center of the labyrinth. They felt it was a special message--an omen. + Note, it was the 13th-- Mary's day.

I looked up mantis in a dictionary and chilled as I discovered mantis comes from the Greek word "prophet." (I've heard that before.) A mantis could also be described as "One inspired by the moon." An insect named for ancient female powers that holds its fore limbs folded, as if in prayer.

I went to my *Animal Speak* book, and it said a praying mantis teaches us that if we go into stillness we can open ourselves to prophecy. Meditating in this way directs the body's life force along specific avenues, strengthening and empowering it through the various organs and systems of the body, which has healing applications. One can learn to use the stillness in varying degrees--whether for creativity or for healing--and this is part of what the praying mantis teaches. + I believe this praying mantis gift from nature was a direct message explaining the purpose of the labyrinth, plus thanking me for recycling the healing funds into this project. A very special message from the heavens.

Robert and helpers cut the pattern of the Chartres

173

Heavenly Text

labyrinth, the pattern from the cathedral in Chartes, France, into the concrete and then filled the cut out pattern with a contrasting concrete. All of this work was done on their hands and knees, and it took about ten days to complete. I was there some part of each day, thoroughly enjoying seeing all take shape. I watched a small piece of ground turn into a beautiful sculptued piece of artwork, later to be enhanced by the landscaping of trees, flowers, and shrubs. I felt proud to be the force behind the project.

September 28, 2004. This night was one of those nights to remember forever. It was the monthly evening that our healing group gets together. When we arrived at our meeting place we could not get into the room. The person with the key did not show. A dozen had showed up and we were debating what to do, when someone said, "Let's go walk the labyrinth." All responded enthusiastically so we took off in our cars to the newly completed labyrinth site. When we began to walk, a beautiful full moon greeted us. + It was radiating its glory next to the big tree on the hill. The scene was perfect. Magnificent! When we finished walking, one of the gals in our group who teaches tai chi said, "Let's do tai chi here on the labyrinth." None of us had ever done the form which she led, but we looked like we had practiced for weeks. The energy was intense. The specialness of the moment was captivating. + I knew in my heart we were blessing the labyrinth, under the full moon, and the process had been arranged from the heavens.

When I got home and called Jane, who had the key to the meeting room, she was embarrassed that she had simply forgotten to attend. Definitely a special + had been created by all of the circumstances. I assured her it was arranged by the angels, and not to feel bad. I was only sorry she had missed

Heavenly Text

such a special encounter.

The next day an e-mail from the person who had led us in the tai chi: "Nancy, Please forward this information to the group regarding the Shibashi form we did last night. Words cannot express how touched I am to have been able to share Shibashi with everyone at the labyrinth. The energy, labyrinth and the night were beautiful. Shibashi emerges from the oriental religion of Taoism which dates back to the 6th century B.C in China. It is a body-prayer that is attuned to cosmic energies. Shibashi uses the natural healing energy in the palm of the hand to send healing blessings to all of creation. The simple harmonizing flow brings awareness of the Sacredness of Life. It helps us to be aware of the Presence of the Creator within us and all around us.

Again, I thought of our praying mantis - the "one inspired by the moon." + "Thanks, God. I appreciate the thanks I am recieving from the heavens for my efforts."

October 13, 2004. I was more than pleased when the hospital picked the 13th for the dedication for the newly installed labyrinth. (Mary's day and a new moon.) The series of circumstances with the moon and this labyrinth adventure defnitely continued throughout the entire process. A huge +.

It rained most of the day but cleared in time for our dedication ceremony. It was cool and terribly windy, but I kept recalling the message from Mary that she is "in the wind." We had a crowd of about 100 in attendance. The dedication was held at sundown, and darkness fell upon us during the ceremony as candles glowed in the background. I gave a short talk; the hospital board of trustee's president gave a short "thank you" talk; Erv sang the "Walking the Labyrinth" song; and all joined in praying a litany of blessings. The dedication

Heavenly Text

was short and very meaningful. I was pleased.

In my talk, I explained the circumstancs of how this labyrinth was literally a dream come true. I told how I began the Labyrinth Association and thanked all for their contributions. I explained how I had buried all the names of the contributors in the heart of the labyrinth. I shared how I have been teaching myself how to bring balance to my body by integrating the heart and mind; how when I live from my heart I become more spiritual. I told that I believe when one becomes more balanced in their spirituality, it is easier to bring balance to the physical body. The labyrinth is an extension of this process, because as one walks the labyrinth in a meditative state it helps to bring harmony and balance to the body, which creates peace within. As individuals become peaceful, it radiates out to the community and out into the world. I see this labyrinth circle as a sacred spot, an ecumenical place where individuals can come together for the sole purpose of creating peace for themselves and others. Peace for all.

I stressed that walking the path is a personal experience, an opportunity to clear the mind and give insight to one's personal journey, to deepen self knowledge, and to empower creativity. I explained how walking it could help one to learn to hear that still small voice inside; that walking it was more than balancing the hemispheres of the brain, it was creating a balance between the two principal aspects of our nature, the physical and the spiritual.

I pray, "Thanks, God, for helping me throughout this journey. I have grown from this experience and know many will benefit from this powerful labyrinth which I know, without a doubt, is blessed from the heavens."

October 27, 2004. The night of the eclipse of the moon. I

Heavenly Text

had a prophetic dream. + I dreamed that Erv and I decided to adopt a new baby. We ordered it and it arrived via UPS in a container that looked like an egg. Pam and Joe were present. Pam touched the egg and it began to crack. Joe touched the egg and it cracked open further. Then a flash, a flame, and a small amount of smoke, and then we could all see this tiny baby inside. So tiny that I wondered how I would feed it and take care of it.

For some reason I ran into the house (I think to get food) and left the baby in the egg container in the front seat of my car. When I came back out, my car had been stolen. I was frantic. Pam and Joe told me not to worry--they knew who stole the car, and we would go to this town called Wicca, and they would point out who took the car and the baby. Pam and Joe insisted that it would be easy to find. I announced that we better hurry, because if the baby didn't eat soon, it would die. End of dream.

Then in early morning when I was lying in bed and meditating I saw human eyes...not like when I have a vision and see the eye...this was different. I saw a pair of eyes and the right eye seemed to have a finger in the corner. + I thanked God for being able to SEE and wondered what this was about. Was it my eye or someone else's?

Was the dream showing me I was experiencing a new birth, changing once again? Or was the baby in the dream about my youngest daughter, Deanna? I have wrote often before that I felt her life's path was preparing her for something great. Was this dream informing me she would also follow in my footsteps? Presently, she is struggling, not understanding what I do.

And for me, it appears another gift is under way. Possibly

Heavenly Text

Spirit was letting me know that in the future I will not only be feeling and hearing, but also seeing problems in the body. I know that true clairvoyance is an awareness when one "sees" and "knows" he is working with the pure action of Spirit. I have been part of the development of senses beyond the ordinary ranges of most humans. My gifts have unfolded in the order that best fits my growth. Visions, prophetic dreams, intuitions, sensings, feeling, hearing and deep compassion are all different, but unique gifts. Yes, there are many energy workers, many medical intuitives, many psychics. However I know unless one unites themselves with Spirit, with the intention of the presence of God, the work is not whole. Thus the Bible's meaning of false prophets.

    As I further thought about the dream, I began reading up on Wicca (on the web) and the dream made even more sense. Wicca is described as follows: To belong to wicca is to be a healer, teacher, seer and giver. Wicca is a belief system of pre-christian traditions, originating from Ireland (28,000 years ago). Wicca has its spiritual roots in the earliest expressions of reverence for nature–mankind--all that is. Reverence for God/Goddess and the belief in reincarnation. (I personally do not have any affilliation with any wicca program but the definition fits with what I believe.)

    I do believe the term Wicca has taken a bad rap over the years since it appears to be the oldest belief system around. It makes sense to me that we humans have strayed far, and Spirit is tempting us back to our original spiritutal roots. Wicca and the term "witchcraft" at the beginning of Christianity were misunderstood. Many were persecuted and killed in order for the new religion, Christianity, to be in control of mankind's thinking. Christianity in its beginning, was a power struggle. Witchcraft and magic were misunderstood. Witchcraft is

Heavenly Text

nothing more than a "craft of the wise." Spirit/energy work could be called magic. Why has mankind gone so far awry? It definitely is time for the masses to return to true spirituality of loving God and their neighbor as themselves. I believe to have a belief in magic means one can create one's dreams, help heal oneself and the world, and find peace in every human heart. It is as simple as that.

I wrote in my journal on the day of the egg dream. I asked what the dream was telling me. I heard very clearly: *"You are like a pebble on the ocean cliff. The water can wash you away. As you get stronger you become the rock--the strong rock that stays. Then you become the cliff, you do not wash away. You change, you become, you are what the energy of the earth makes you. We are making you a cliff."*

I pray, "Thanks, God, for my journey and the gifts along the way. I better understand past dreams of the rocks. My life has certainly had its rocky times and certainly Deanna has had hers. You have guided us. You have let me know that my husband, children, and grandchildren have all helped in my spiritual evolution. Yes, truly we are all one, all needing each other, all of the time. As I have evolved, my family is evolving. We are all like the labyrinth with its many twists and turns, reaching the center only to reach out further -- to our families, to the communty, to the world. I remember you saying your visions were for guidance for the writing of Your book. Does this mean these writings are nearing completion and release to the world? Thanks, God, for the gift of knowing your ways. Lead me and guide me. I AM yours. "

***

Heavenly Text

I have learned that salvation, eternity, is not given to us. It has to be earned. Mankind has become complacent and adopted the status quo instead of searching for the mysteries of life. Life is like the game of "Clue" - solving the mystery. Each of us individually needs to search the unknown to discover our true self. I believe Jesus did not come "to save us" but simply, "to show the way." We each have to do our part, just as Jesus did. Jesus told us, "Become like a child." For me, this means to seek the unknown in order to discover the "truth" and "self." For years, I have been seeking and discovering these mysteries. Each year has peeled away another layer.

I believe the present teachings of Christianity do not teach individuals to reach for the unfoldment of the mysteries. Fear and punishment are taught instead of spiritual evolution and rebirth. Thus, most individuals are afraid in life and of death. This needs to change.

As I've gone through life's education, I've come to understand and know more than I ever dreamed possible. By uniting my mind with Spirit I've blossomed into a being that I did not know I could be. As the world rapidly changes before us, maybe a small portion of what I share will help others along their way. I believe God is using me as a bridge for Christians to help awaken lost thoughts and hidden knowledge. I know my visions come from heaven. If one wishes to dismiss visions as madness, one would have to reject all Christian visionaries throughout time.

The Gift of Patience

It's been a little over a year since I've written in my manuscript but I again feel Spirit's push. It appears this manuscript is not yet finished or Spirit is waiting for everything and everyone to move into its proper place? It seems to be again the time for learning patience.

February 13, 2005. Information was relayed to me during the night in a series of three dreams. I awoke during the night from the first dream and remembered that I had dreamed about the web address "108.com." I had never seen anything like that on the computer before, so I thought, "How strange!" I fell asleep and again had a dream about a computer site "108.com." When I woke I wondered why that dream had repeated itself. Again I drifted back to sleep. Suddenly I was awakened by a jolt and saw "108.com." I said, "OK, OK, I'll go type that number into my computer; but I know I've never seen an internet site consisting of only numbers."

When I entered "108.com" into the computer, I was dumbfounded when the screen filled with pictures of a man (guru/yogi) from India, meditating and writing. + I knew a powerful message was being relayed to me, but why? I noticed from information provided on the site that this gentleman was going to be in Hawaii on one of his world trips, speaking of his beliefs in his God (Lord Krishna). (Christ in Hinduism) I looked for further info on that web site and found a link to

Heavenly Text

another web site. This took me to a site in Calcutta, India. (PureBhakti.com) which means devotion to the Supreme Lord. I read the lengthy site all morning. I learned the picture I saw at "108.com" was Sri Srimad Bhaktivedana Narayana Gosvami Mhahraji, who has written many books and gives talks worldwide as a servant for God.

I became very curious about the significance of this information and wondered why I had received the prompting from the heavens to be introduced to this. It seemed that Spirit was sending me further and further back into history, letting me know all is one, all is working together-- always has been and always will be.

I called a friend to pull up the web site, and we discussed the pictures. She remarked, "I think it means you are supposed to do the same thing: write more and lecture." Chills abounded. Realizing it was the 13th that I received this information, There was a place on the site for an e-mail so I sent the following message:

I had a repeated dream seeing the web address "108.com." I often receive visions during the night and have prophetic dreams, so I considered it a "God Message" and went to my computer. You can imagine how shocked I was when your site loaded. Does this happen often? Do you hear from others in this manner? I have read your web page for several hours and am very curious why Spirit wanted me to know of Bhakti Yoga. I am 63 years old. I have a healing ministry in my home, using alternative and complementary healing techniques. I feel God's power guiding my hands, and at times, witness miracles. Over the past fifteen years I have kept a journal of my spiritual evolution. Possibly, if you meditate on my name, you will be given further information to help me solve this spiritual message and why it has lead me to you. Thank you. Nancy

Return message: Hare Krishna Nancy, I am very happy to read your letter and how you came to find our web site. Bhakti yoga is the

Heavenly Text

eternal religion of the soul. It is not sectarian and everyone is invited and welcome with open arms to study these teachings, which can lead us to the highest happiness. Certainly mystic revelation can indicate the path toward God. Why not? Vedic scriptures describe the nature of the "supersoul," which is a portion of the Supreme Lord's energy which resides with the soul in every living being. The Vedas compare the soul and the Supersoul to two friendly birds sitting on the same tree. One of the birds (the individual atomic soul) is eating the fruit of the tree, and the other bird (Krishna) is simply watching His friend. Of these two birds -- although they are the same in quality -- one is captivated by the fruits of the material tree, while the other is simply witnessing the activities of His friend. Sometimes the supersoul will communicate to the soul, which is probably how you received the intuition to come to 108.com, which is affiliated with PureBhakti.com I hope you will find our site interesting, and if I can help in any way, please let me know, Kishore Krishna Dasa

After reading this all I could think of was my many bird communications and experiences. I remembered the two hawks on the one branch when I went to Minnesota in 1997, and the two hawks on one branch when we returned from our grandson's funeral in 1999. I knew without a doubt I was now dealing with another very profound +.

I decided to go back to the "108.com" site to see the pictures again and the pictures were no longer there. I called my friend and she could not get them back on the screen either. In fact "108.com" is a web site for radio communications. What I had seen earlier was nowhere to be found. (Now, that was really a weird feeling--I am glad that I had a witness. Although the "108.com" was no longer accessible, the Bhakti site still was.)

I looked up the word Bhakti in the Bhagava-Gita, translated by Barbara Miller, and discovered it derives from

Heavenly Text

Sanskit root bhaj "to share," from which is also derived the word bhagavat, "Lord," referring to Lord Krishna as the object of devotion who shares in the life of his devotee. This devotion enables one to engage actively in the world and still have spiritual freedom. Through devotion, the self expands toward the infinite, and the infinite is brought to a conceivable human scale.

The aim of Bhakti yoga is to direct toward God, the love that lies at the base of every heart thru devoted service. To the Bhakti, feelings are more important than thoughts and their love of God is their first choice in life. (This is exactly what Christ taught.)

Yoga derives from the Sanskit root yui, "to yoke." In the Gita it is the yoking of oneself to Krishna's divine purpose, the spiritual and physical discipline that integrates aspects of reality. One who practices discipline is called a man of discipline - a yogi.

More research taught me that the number 108 is a very ancient revered number in the East, thought to represent the feminine principle. There are 108 beads on the Hindu Rosary (japa malas), and there are 108 beads that hang around KwanYins' neck. So after many hours of searching and reading, I know that the prompting did indeed come from Mother Mary and I was being told that my life mirrors Bhakti yoga. On further contemplation, I have also come to the realization that the basic principles of Bhakti are richly exemplified in Christianity. God always was and always will be, and ancient generations are no different than today.

Was I also being prompted to share my writings? Was I being told to put the messages on the web? The feminine aspect of nature was on the move nudging me on.

Heavenly Text

Back on May 24, 2002, when I had a vision of a jigsaw puzzle box, and on the cover of the box I could see steps. As the steps became clearer, I realized the steps were the steps on a pyramid. The top-the capstone of the pyramid-was missing. I thought at the time the vision was telling me that I was piecing the puzzle together and the best was yet to come. Now in 2005, I better understand that vision, as I believe I have pieced more of the puzzle's total picture together.

I recently read *The Galactic Alignment* written by John Major Jenkins, and now realize that vision in 2002 was the Kukulcan pyramid at Chichen Itza (constructed in 8 AD), which is said to encode the progression of the universe. This pyramid does not have an apex and has steps just like I saw in my vision. Every year, at the time of the Earth's equinoxes a "shadow serpent" appears and slithers down the Northern stairway- caused by the orientation of the pyramid to the late afternoon sun which makes the pyramid a procession star clock. For centuries, many have believed that this points to an upcoming, significant astronomical event - a time when the Earth will be in the exact center of the Milky Way in direct alignment with the Sun and Pleiades, predicted to occur in December 2012. (Pleiades is the world head point of the world axis.)

I have read several times that the earth is aligning with the solstice axis, the galactic center, and the sun. Exact alignment of the solstices and equinoxes with the Milky Way (the center of the universe) occur every 26,000 years and it is believed this stimulates consciousness. This cycle of time is the amount of time for the constellations of the zodiac to complete one cycle of movement across the heavens. These 26,000 procession cycles are recorded in many ancient civilizations and traditions including Vedic, Egyptian, and Mayan. These cycles are

Heavenly Text

understood as a vast collective spiritual gestation for humanity - a time of spiritual and social transformation. In other words, the changing of the galaxy changes us, which offers an understanding of the Vedic statement, "As above, so below."

Spirit was definitely conveying another important message. + It had taken me three years to figure out this vision. Is this serpent on the Chichen Itza pyramid mirroring the human Kundalini? Is this a place depicting the importance of the joining of the male and female? Was Chichen Itza built by beings of a higher intelligence to give us a time schedule for the evolution of consciousnes - the birth of humanity's higher mind? I now believe so.

For me, astrologically speaking, Chichen Itza appears to be another example for mankind from the heavens, demonstrating the importance of Kundalini (the serpent), the importance of balance, not only of humans but the universe. It appears the processes and patterns in the sky seem to parallel, or reflect, the earth, as it does in mankind. Furthermore, the date of December 21, 2012 is the date that the Mayan Calendar ends. I find this all fascinating!

Jenkins also mentions that a man named LaVioletter predicted years ago that a burst of energy would emanate from the galaxy center before this alignment took place causing the earth to change on its axis. We have been told that the tsunami of December 2004 did exactly that. Will there be more tilts of the axis that will align or change things? Time will tell, as well as the serpent on the pyramid at Chichen Itza.

I now know and believe, without a doubt, it is time for the masses of the world to realize we are living at a profound time in the history of mankind. As I have written before: it is a time of major change. We need to ready ourselves for this

Heavenly Text

transformation: a new awakening of consciousness, a new cleansing of our Earth. I know Spirit has been conveying this to me with my visions and spiritual experiences. Spirit has been using me as a messenger for this world phenomena. I now believe the human spiritual anatomy is a microcosmic reflection of the universe on a larger scale. The galactic alignment will usher in this new period-this New Age. We are being prepared for this gift from the heavens in many ways. The significance of this time has also been heralded by Mother Mary's visits to the Earth. I vividly remember reading many times in Mary's messages, "Do you not know of the times you are living in?" The ancients believed the Milky Way represented Isis, the feminine nature of the universe. Is Mother Mary our present day Isis as the Earth enters the center of the Milky Way?

I know the balance of the male and female brings about a higher evolution of mankind. I also have since learned that the symbol of the Ouroboros, which I saw in a dream in August 2003, is a mythic symbol for the Milky Way. (Myth refers to the serpent of light residing in the heavens as representation of completed cycles.) I wrote at the time that I thought the dream was telling me I had balanced the male and female - completed a cycle. Many others are also presently coming into this alignment. In every living creature there is the striving towards divine unity--balancing the male and female--the two forms of creative forces. All of creation needs to come into balance in order to bring balance to our planet. The Earth is doing likewise, coming into balance by releasing negative vibrations with hurricanes, earthquakes, volcanic eruptions, storms, etc.

No wonder the lengthy vision of December 23, 2000, ended with an astrological clock. + Spirit was telling me to watch the astrological signs that were pointing to the end of a

Heavenly Text

cycle in the universe, plus it was indicating the importance of a change in me. I now know seeing "the Eye," the "Star of David," and "the Pyramid" was indicting the importance of balancing the male and female. (Also I've since realized that the pyramid image seems to be a wireless energy transmission from the heavens to our wave length of consciousness). In that same vision, I saw a dove turning the pages of a book, which I now know was telling me that my life was a reflection of the book of life, and I was being asked to continue to write about it.

That vision even occurred on December 23, a day close to the date indicated by the Mayan Calendar as the beginning of a New Age. (Huge +) That vision was preceded by the audible voice a few weeks before on December 8, 2000, when I heard, *"Nancy are you sure because after thi,s there is no turning back."* I now believe I was being told that I was going to be reprogrammed and that I had an important job - to tell the world that we as humans will determine our own fate and the outcome of December 21, 2012. It is up to us to become balanced, to love one another, and to help balance the Earth. We each need to pay attention to our individual "+'s." Balancing the power within us is not an option, but a command. Will the date of December 21 be "the moment in time" (spoken of at the apparition sites), when all will experience a deep inner knowing of where they stand in the eyes of God?

I was prompted to reread my manuscript which I had not done for some time. I was shocked to discover the writings in the end of the manuscript seemed to mirror much of the front of the manuscript. It now makes sense that many of my earlier visions and dreams were preparing me for what was to come.

Heavenly Text

I've since read that our DNA is code that becomes our reality. I now realize that is exactly what appeared to happen. I now believe that in our DNA are encoded messages (which are possible to access) that propel us to quest for our truths to complete our missions.

August 9, 2005. I had a dream in which I saw myself lift a book from a shelf. On the cover of the book I read "Descartes." I heard, *"Buy this and read it"*. +

The next day I searched and found there were many titles to choose from because Descartes was a prolific writer. I debated which one to buy. I purchased his most famous book, *Meditations on First Philosophy*.

Descartes (1596-1650) was a deep thinker, who reminded me of myself, in that he constantly analyzed, processed, doubted and questioned himself and his thoughts until he reached conclusions that resonated. Descartes was before his time, and the church did not approve of his writings. He wrote about the existence of God, gave arguments for reincarnation, cause and effect, and much, much, more. When I read, "mans life discovery is based on what is discovered before" it reminded me of my comments above.

In this discourse, Descartes wrote the philosophical argument that God exists, and the mind is distinct from the body. He wrote, "There is within me an idea of something more perfect than me, it follows this thing really exists." To me, this is the Christ consciousness within that I know to be true.

I loved his statement: "I have no right to complain that the part God has wished me to play is not the principal and most perfect one of all." (I bet Jesus would agree with that statement. He followed through with what He knew He was

Heavenly Text
instructed to do and I'm trying to do the same.)
("Thanks, God, definitely these were messages for me. I realize that I do not always understand the role You have laid out for me by sending me visions, dreams and intuitive insights into Your ways. Descartes words helped remind me that I need to understand all people will not perceive as I do, because they have not experienced what I have experienced. I know You continue to prepare me to be strong and firm in what I know to be true. I know it may take awhile for others to understand what I know.")

September 3, 2005. In a dream I saw a space vehicle flying in the distance. It looked like a shuttle. It flew lower and lower, came closer and closer, changed to a spiral shape and then landed in a nearby tree top. Then a huge butterfly immerged from it and came and landed on my head. + I took hold of the butterfly and said, "I'm not letting go of you. You are beautiful. You are mine." Knowing that a butterfly is a symbol of metamorphosis or transformation, I was filled with joy and great expectation.

The next day I processed the dream. The *Animal Speaks* book says the butterfly is a symbol in myth and religion -- a symbol of the soul. I believe I was being informed that I have reached another level of transformation. Am I going to be experiencing joy on another level? Is change coming again?

October 13, 2005. I received an early morning phone call from Sabra saying, "They just called and are delivering the sculpture." I jumped in my car and rushed to the Labyrinth site. It was just over a year before that I had taken Sabra Meyer, a local artist, to the Labyrinth to see whether she was interested in sculpting a piece for the site. Then, as she walked

Heavenly Text

across the concrete she held up her hands and said, "I see a circle being held up by hands." I chilled and said, "Hold that thought. That sounds wonderful." She followed with, "I believe this ground was once my great grandfather's." (Chills abounded again. It appeared a circle in her life was being completed, as was one in my life.)

It was now one year later, and I witnessed them putting in the sculpture. I was stunned with the beauty and simplicity of the piece. I was thrilled that it had arrived on Mary's special day. I felt this was indeed a "thank you" from Spirit. Even a bigger thank you came when the hospital dedicated the sculpture as a memorial in my daughter Pam's name, along with a deceased hospital employee. Later sitting at the dedication, gazing at the sculpture, an interior voice said, *"Nancy, don't you get it? Your hands created this circle."* + Chills abounded. I knew in my heart that Spirit had whispered in Sabra's ear that day when she and I first visited the Labyrinth site. She did not know of my hands-on ministry.

("Thanks, God. What a wonderful thank you. Indeed, my life has completed a circle-from Pam to the Labyrinth-a circle that I would never have dreamed possible back when I gave her back to You in 1983. I also now understand that the vortex of energy changes at a Labyrinth site, for the community, and for all those who walk it. Thank you for encouraging me to put one here in Columbia. I hope to be instrumental in putting in more.")

December 25, 2005. In a dream I was in a house on a beach watching a cat using its paw and tail to draw a picture in the sand. The picture ended up being a huge fish. + Then a huge grasshopper came up to me. I picked it up. After a time the grasshopper let me know it wanted to be put down and I let it go.

Upon awaking I knew that the symbol of the fish represented Jesus. I concurred the dream was a message from Him. I also remembered a book cover that has a picture of someone drawing a Labyrinth in the sand. Was I being told those walking the Labyrinth would learn to hear His voice better?

The Animal Speak book says the grasshopper is a symbol encouraging one to leap forward. I read that by moving their legs in different directions the grasshopper is able to locate a sound source. It stated that this connection between sensing sound and the legs is highly significant. The Labyrinth does wind and turn in different directions.

("Thanks God. A message for all to trust their inner voice when walking the Labyrinth. A powerful encouraging message. I also presume we are getting ready for another leap forward. I await in joyful anticipation.")

January 5, 2006. Having fought a nine month long battle with lung cancer, my dear friend and spiritual comrade M.L. died this week. I'm sure she is soaring with the angels and very, very, happy to be home. I will miss her terribly. She was such an inspiration to me and many others. We had many meaningful phone conversations during her illness. I asked her if I could use her real name in my writings and she told me not to, explaining, "Please just use M.L. as we have previously discussed. I think it will be better for my family." Although I would love to give her personal credit I will respect her wishes.

One of her last messages to me was "I see you walking the Labyrinth with six blue birds following along behind you like little ducklings." + I wonder who the six are? I'm sure in time I will know.

Heavenly Text

The day M.L. departed this earth, I experienced a very unusual day of releasing energy in my body. Later, when I heard it was the day she died, I wondered if in some way our energetic connection was the reason for my releases. I know we are all one, and she and I were deeply connected.

("Thanks, God, for sending M.L. into my life and sharing her direct phone line to You. I know I now have another angel in heaven. I look forward to being reunited with her one of these days, although I'm sure she is still very near.")

January 27, 2006. In a vision someone offered me a water glass full of beautiful berries. I heard, *"Eat these and you will not get the bird flu."* + ("Thanks, God. Is this a message for me or many?") I looked up information on berries and discovered they help build the immune system. Interesting! (Much later I read that a research had shown that elderberries helped fight the bird flu.)

April 3, 2006. In a dream, I saw a basket sitting on top of a chest of drawers. Inside of the basket, I could see a University of Missouri tiger mascot outfit. Suddenly the tiger outfit started moving and I saw a cat crawl out from underneath it. Then just as quickly, the cat pulled the outfit back over its head and slowly scooted backwards back into the basket. + I asked, "Now, how did you do that?" I woke up.

As I thought about the dream the next few days I believe it was telling me that I live here in Columbia, home of the MU Tigers, and that is where I am to stay as I work for Mother Mary. The cat was nestled in a basket, a symbol for the womb of the earth, and when the cat tried to come out, it knew to return. Or was the cat telling me it is time to come out and stay out and go forward? Whatever the answer I do know I am to

Heavenly Text
fulfill my destiny here in Columbia.

May 27, 2006. I was thrilled to receive a vision, as it had been awhile. As the bright circle opened, I saw a large book, with gentle moving hands laid upright on it. Then a huge branch of green leaves began to appear beside the book and hands. + I questioned, "Is that my book? My hands? Is the book about finished? What are the green leaves about?" The vision faded away.

I spent hours, then days, trying to figure out its entire meaning. Is it time for mature leaves to come forth?

June 12, 2006. I was administering Spirit/energy work to someone when she suddenly said, "I am seeing the most beautiful scene." I asked if she wanted to share. She replied, "I see this huge branch full of blossoms, and the wind is gently blowing them off. I see a background of a very gorgeous colorful sunset as they slowly float thru the air to the ground." + (I know when a client gets a message it is for both of us and this time I knew this one was definitely for me.) I recalled my dream back in August 1991. In that dream I vomited and saw birds pick up the vomit and place it on branches on the tree. The vomit then turned into blossoms. I then heard the word "proliferate," over and over. At that time, I realized I was to write and my words would turn into blossoms. Now the blossoms were falling. Tears flowed as I recalled the leaves in my earlier vision and realized I was being told mature leaves were coming forth.

June 18, 2006. As I drifted off to sleep I asked over and over for a dream to help me to better know what my mission in the future would be. I heard several times +*"You are to help*

Heavenly Text
balance the earth with the heavens."
I thought of my life, my writings, my healing ministry, my Labyrinth. All the things that I have been doing but yet I must need to do more.
("What God, what? Lead the way.")

June 21, 2006. I met another individual who is a spiritual seer. When we were sharing experiences, she said, "I don't know what you are doing, but you certainly have a lot of help. I see many individuals around you: Mary, Jesus, lots of saints, including Jude, Francis of Assisi, and others. + What do you do?"

My heart melted. How did she know? I decided she must be a true seer. I told her I was writing a book for the heavens. We discussed it at length.

The next morning she called and said, "As I left your house St. Dominic came to me and asked why I didn't tell you he was also with you. Then this morning when I woke up, St. Dominic again spoke to me and said, Call Nancy and tell her to read about me."

Excited, I googled St. Dominic on the computer and read the whole morning. I was especially curious because I knew the Newman Center was getting a new pastor. Two Dominican priests were coming in July to help out the small number of priests in our diocese.

I read that St. Dominic was the saint to whom Mary had appeared, who helped promote the rosary. In reading, I also quickly learned that St. Dominic's feast day is my birthday. (Surprise!) And I was really surprised when I read that St. Dominic had a vision of a man with whom he was supposed to work. He did not know who he was. When he later met the man, it was St. Francis of Assisi. Together, they started the religious orders of friars to spread God's word.

Fascinating! Is one of these new priests the one God wants me to work with? Could one of them be the person I saw in the vision in October two years ago? Could there be a correlation between St. Dominic's life and mine? Is this the reason for the vision of the mature green leaves? Many thoughts and questions ran through my mind. I could hardly wait for the new priests to arrive.

July 2, 2006. We made a trip to Kentucky to visit Mom and attend a family reunion. Mother is still hanging on. She is now 90 and still at the convent. She just can't seem to let go. She is pitiful. Her mind is much worse. She does know us by name, but there is not much conversation. She generally sits in her chair, her head hanging down with eyes closed. This visit she didn't talk much and would just grunt when asked questions. Although all nine of her children were there, she wasn't part of the gathering.

This trip was especially burdensome for me because we visited others who were sick. Not only were we with Mom, but we also visited her brother, my Uncle Gene, who has cancer and was recovering from surgery; and we visited Mom's sister my Aunt Sissy who had just discovered she had terminal cancer. It appears this generation of family is quickly fading away.

July 26, 2006. My dear friend Lisa C. was here. We exchanged Spirit/energy work. She remarked that I looked tired. I told her how fatigued I had been since returning from Kentucky. I replied, "I suppose I just took on too much from too many that are sick and from many who do not know they are sick." Lisa knows that I feel other's problems in my body.

Heavenly Text

Usually I can handle it without complaint, but this trip really did me in. It was taking me longer to recover because I was also trying to catch up on backlogged appointments. I said to Lisa, "It's time to rest for awhile. I guess I sometimes push to hard. Thanks for reminding me to slow down."

Lisa replied, + "Stop talking. I see Jesus. He is here. Go get your manuscript. I'll explain later." I ran downstairs wondering what was happening. When I returned she took my manuscript and turned it over to the back side. She explained, "I saw Jesus with a book. He turned it over to the back and turned back three pages and pointed to a paragraph. I asked what book and He turned it over. I saw it was your manuscript, with your name on it." +

Needless to say, I was surprised and thrilled. We immediately went to the paragraph she had been shown by Jesus and were astonished that He had pointed to a paragraph He had given Sister Joseta Menendez. +"*There are many souls who urged on by the hope of salvation but still more by the motive of love, are resolute in their determination to follow Me in the way of the cross. They eagerly embrace the perfect life and devote themselves to My service in order to carry, not part of the cross, but the whole of it. Their one desire is to relieve and comfort Me. They offer themselves for all My will may ask of them and seek out all that may give Me pleasure. They think neither of reward nor of their own merits, nor of the fatigues and sufferings that may occur to them, their one object being to show Me their love and console My heart.*"

Tears flowed from both of us. A perfect message. We knew we were hearing straight from Jesus. This was probably the strongest message we'd ever received. Jesus pointing to the exact paragraph to affirm our conversation. Wow! I recalled the Bhatki message.

Heavenly Text
("Thanks, God. Moments like these are what make all I do worthwhile. I recall how many years ago I wrote that I could never be like Sister Menedez. Times do change. I know You were letting me know that I have learned how to give of myself, as she did, in order to help others.")

July 30, 2006. A little before 4am I was awakened with a pain in my chest. I wondered who I was sharing energy with. Then I experienced one of those strong electrical shocks that I often get. + I thanked Spirit for whatever was taking place. Soon I went back to sleep.

The next morning Aunt Martha called and said Aunt Sissy had died a little before 5am. (Different time zones so the same time.) I again realized my body was helping to release someone who was dying. (This happens often.) This time someone I deeply loved. Aunt Sissy had been so supportive of my work and what I do. We had experienced a miracle five years earlier. I'll explain.

Aunt Sissy and Aunt Martha came as my surrogate mothers for my 60th birthday croning in 2001. The night before they arrived I had experienced lots of uncomfortable sensations in my body as I kept hearing over and over, "cauterizing...cauterizing." When they arrived I saw that Aunt Sissy had two blue fingers due to bad circulation. The doctor had told her to not travel. She had ignored his warning and came to be with me. I worked on her, balancing her body. We witnessed the correct color returning to her fingers. When she returned home the doctor could not believe it. He ran tests anyway but all was fine. At the time I had wondered if I was helping her or she was helping me. I thought a lot about generational healing. Now I wondered again: Was part of me leaving or was she leaving me part of her energy? Is she part

Heavenly Text

of my soul group? Is this why I was so tired upon my return from Kentucky-because I was sharing in her departure? A lot to think about.

August 6, 2006. Lisa C. and I were together. I was working on her when she said, "I see a golden Light hovering over us." + I replied, "What is it trying to tell us?" Lisa kept saying, "I'm not getting anything." I kept hearing, *"Open your mouth,"* so I told her to open her mouth. Nothing happened. I heard again, *"Open your mouth. Let it come out."* Still nothing. Then I wondered if the message could mean me? I opened my mouth and a voice came through me, + *"My daughters, the Holy Spirit is overshadowing you. I will be with you. I bestow my peace upon you. Go forth with my graces and blessings as you do My work. I love you."*

Lisa said, "Wow! The bright golden Light left the second the words stopped. That was something else." I agreed and said, "Never have I done something like that." Lisa said, "It didn't sound like you either."

We both were in awe and went from tears to laughter as we knew we had heard His "Word" - communicated to us through sight and sound. Again, another amazing experience.

("Thanks, God. What a wonderful joyful spiritual encounter.")

August 10, 2006. My sister informed the family that Mom was much worse. I meditated and felt Spirit was telling me Mom was dying. I called Lisa and asked her to check in on Mom. Lisa said, "Three of your Mom's chakras are dark. Yes, you're right. I believe she is dying. She probably won't live to the weekend."

I decided to go home. Erv went with me and we stayed at

Heavenly Text

Aunt Marney's. When Aunt Martha and I went over the next morning to see Mom she was in a stupor, slumped in her chair. I held her hand and she began to jerk and jump, never opening her eyes. Martha asked, "What is going on?" I replied, "I don't know. She is either letting go or trying to not let go. I'm not sure." I held her hand for over an hour as we witnessed her body jumping and jerking. I kept hearing, + *"Trust Me,"* *"Trust Me."*

At noon, some nurses came in to take her to the bathroom before lunch. As they lifted her she cried out and slumped over. I thought she was at last letting go. They then put her in bed. She was as white as the sheet and her hair. Martha and I sat beside her for a couple of hours and she never moved. (I felt sorry for Martha witnessing within two weeks another sister dying.) I kept telling Mom it was all right to go home. I could see spirits around her and felt they were coming to get her. After awhile I finally said, "I think we should go." Martha said, "Don't you think we should stay?" I assured her mother did not know we were there, so we might as well go.

The next morning we returned. Mom still lay in an almost coma-like sleep. I tried to wake her over and over but she never budged. After a few hours, we again decided to go. I called Lisa again and she said all of Mom's chakras were black except one, and she thought Mom would be dead by morning.

The next morning, when we walked into Mom's room we could hardly believe what we saw. Mom was sitting in her chair, her head up with both eyes open (usually her right eye is closed) and carrying on a conversation. She was better than we have seen her in a couple of years. All were amazed who saw her. When I called Lisa that night she said, "I know, I know. I checked on your Mom this morning and I could not believe it. All her chakras were lit up again. I've never seen anything like

Heavenly Text

this." I told Lisa, "I think Mom might have had a near death experience or something. She is so different. Only she and God know!"

I wondered if she had drawn energy from me to stay here for awhile. I constantly wonder why she cannot let go and go home. That generational healing thing again? Am I helping her or is she helping me? I put it all in God's hands.

Later that day, Erv and I decided to come home to Missouri. The continued reports from home are that she is still holding her own, but starting to have her ups and downs again. Time will tell.

August 29, 2006. I met with Father Thomas, our new Dominican pastor and explained to him that I was writing a book for God. (He had arrived in July but I waited a few months before approaching him for a private visit.) I told him that I have a healing ministry in my home. He asked me to tell him about it. He was very receptive, thoughtful, and interested as I told him about my visions, prophetic dreams, healings, etc. He asked if he could come sometime and see what I do. I was thrilled that again I finally had a priest who was interested in my journey. He asked to read my manuscript. When we finished our conversation I was humbled when he asked if I would pray over him. I vividly remembered how nervous I had been ten years ago when Jesus had told me to pray over Father Mike. This time I was at peace. I placed my hands on Father Thomas's head and thanked God for bringing him to me.

When I finished praying, Father Thomas put his arms around my shoulders and said, "I'll be happy to walk this journey with you." I was delirious with joy and excitement. At last, after 15 years, God had sent the person I am to work with. I can't prove it but I do believe he is the one I saw in the

Heavenly Text

vision (Oct. 2004). Alleluia! I didn't tell him that. I'll wait until he reads my manuscript.

Could it be that because Fr. Thomas was a Southern Baptist, became a Catholic, then a priest, that he is more open to change? I believe so. God had sent the perfect person. I wonder what the future holds for us. The man in my vision did look older, but I still believe this is he, so maybe it will be a while but that's fine too. I've learned long ago that God's time is not the same as my time.

October 17, 2006. This night I had a very interesting dream. + Another car dream. My car wouldn't start and I was trying to get help. I approached some men who were playing golf and asked them if they had cables to start a car. They said they didn't, but they could push my car over to the hill assuring me that when I went down the hill there was a good possibility the car would jump start itself. After they pushed my car to the top of the hill I looked and was surprised to see not a normal hill but a concrete tunnel with steps going down. I became concerned that it would be too dangerous to drive the car down the steps. I knew I'd never done that. I asked my daughter who was with me to get out of the car in case I had a wreck. I was sitting behind the wheel mustering my courage, wondering if the brakes would work on steps when I suddenly awakened. I was shocked to be in my bed. The dream had seemed so real. My heart was beating rapidly.

I tried to interpret the message from Spirit. I know cars in my dreams are always about my personal transportation in life. Was going forward, down the steps, going to be dangerous, fast, seem out of control? Or was the dream simply encouraging me to take more steps? Or was the dream more about Deanna taking steps? Or was I being reminded how hard

Heavenly Text
the journey has been all along? Probably some of all.

December 27, 2006. What a wonderful Christmas season. I could hardly believe my ears when Deanna said she wanted to learn Spirit/energy work. + This last year she has been letting me work on her and the grandchildren and is finally understanding how wonderful Spirit/energy can be. Even her husband Jeff let me work on him. Ten years ago he was saying what I did was of the devil. Obviously, he did not understand.

I'll explain: When I first started going to apparition sites, Jeff kept telling Deanna that those things were of the devil. His fundamental background had given him a very narrow view of Mary. He told her "Even a Spirit of darkness can appear as light." He encouraged Deanna not to even talk to me about it. And she didn't-which hurt deeply. When my energy work started he was convinced I was working with negative forces, so when we were together what I did with my life was never mentioned. As you remember, Erv's Christian background also had created a doubtful view so there was a heavy strain between us for many years. But time and example has finally turned the tide. I kept reminding myself, "They will know you by your fruits."

Deanna's neighbor, a chiropractor, encouraged Deanna to go to a female chiropractor friend of his who worked with allergies. One day Deanna went to the lady chiropractor and called me exclaiming, "Mom, you are going to think I am crazy but I went to someone today who had me hold my arm out and ask questions of my body." I replied, "You mean kinesiology?" Shocked that I knew what she was talking about she said, "You know about that?" (Kinesiology is a simple muscle testing technique used as a diagnostic tool. When the conscious mind has a belief that is in conflict with a formerly

Heavenly Text

learned truth stored in the subconscious mind, the intellectual conflict expresses itself as a weakening of the body's muscles.)

Thus began the opening of the door. Our conversations slowly evolved into talks about the many alternative techniques that I've worked with for years. Over time she told the female chiropractor that I did energy work and the doctor encouraged Deanna to let me work on her. Once that happened it was fine for me to work on the grandchildren and even Jeff stepped forward. God does work in mysterious ways, but sometimes slowly. This took ten years. A very hard time for me.

("Thanks, God. We have come a long way. You are proving to me how when one changes others follow.")

January 3, 2007. I had a long talk with the other Dominican priest, Father Joachim. When I mentioned apparition sites he immediately said, "I believe in them. I've been to Medjugorje twice." I began telling him about my experinces. He also was very accepting. What a difference a few years make. Suddenly, I seem to be supported from all sides. Father Joachim asked to read my manuscript and when he read it he did some editing.

("Thanks, God. I'm so joyful witnessing and sharing the mature leaves coming forth. Thanks for sending me another priest.)

February 13, 2007. This day I watched Oprah. She was endorsing the book *The Secret*, which explains how our thoughts create our reality. Then that night I had a dream in which several of us were discussing the book. I suggested that we all should think "I want to see Jesus." I immediately heard, *"No, that's your job."* + So I started praying asking to see Jesus. All of a sudden I saw a huge bright oval Light and Jesus

Heavenly Text

stepped out. + I was in awe. A powerful dream and again on the thirteenth!

("Thanks, God. You have definitely proven to me many times how our thoughts create our reality but this was extra special.")

After my and Lisa's powerful experience of hearing God's word last August, she decided to go forth by relocating. She moved out west to Arizona because she had been receiving promptings to do so for some time. (If intersted in knowing more about Lisa visit her web site expansiveawareness.com)

Since being there she has attended a workshop by Richard Bartlett. She called, excited, saying, "You need to go to this guy's web page. I attended his workshop and he is wonderful. I witnessed him doing instant healings. He calls what he does 'transformation of matrix energy'."

I immediately went to the site and I ordered his book. I was thrilled to find a comrade who could explain what I have been saying and doing. "Thanks, God, again for guiding us. Lisa followed through with your guidance and has relayed very important information to me that I feel you want in this manuscript. Now I'm going to follow through by writing about holograms and matrix energetics."

I read Bartlett's book, *Matrix Energetics*, I had recently just finished reading others, - *The Holographic Universe* by Talbot, - *The Divine Matrix* by Braden. All are physicists and scientists sharing their thoughts on a new paradigm - a holographic Universe. They all explain a hologram as a three dimensional image that looks life-like when projected or exposed by direct light. Each fragment of the whole is also a hologram - each part is in the whole and the whole is within

Heavenly Text

each part. In these books I read about quantum physics, morphic fields, photons, and the energy matrix. Bartlett says, "Matrix energy is based on laws of physics, concepts and laws of quantum physics, and Morphic Resonance."

Their information seems to be the scientific answers to my many questions and is helping to bring more pieces of the puzzle together. I'm better understanding how science is beginning to understand and explain that all is information and Light. Science now realizes that it appears that a force, a field, a presence links us all together. For me, holograms could be the answer. Jesus says, "The Father is in me and I am in the Father." According to the holographic principle we are all connected. Could this be the explanation of the spark of God that resides in each of us?

It's fact that the holographic principle has been proven in our DNA. Every small part of our body is a mirror of the whole body. So it makes sense to me that this is how consciousness is also connected - by holograms. If a part cannot be separated from the whole, and reality mirrors itself, it seems feasible that eventually everything would reach a state of complete self-knowing.

In Genesis, it says we are made in the image and likeness of God-(a hologram?) I have not heard the church address this new principle of holograms but I believe it is the explanation for healings. The information and Light is everywhere, within us all the time. We just need to use it. I know and believe that if our heart's intention matches that of God we become co-creators with God. The universe responds to our belief.

Anything that has ever happened can happen again. It is out there ready to be tapped into. Therefore a change anywhere is a change everywhere. As Gregg Braden says, "What we see

Heavenly Text

in our universe is really us-our individual and collective minds -transforming the possibilities of the deeper realms into physical reality."

Back to the premise I've always declared-we all can do the work of Jesus, if we love God and our neighbor as ourselves. It matters not to which religion or spiritual culture one belongs. The ancients down to the present have always been showing the way. Krishna taught total love and service. Buddha taught wisdom, compassion, and oneness. Christ taught us how to combine all. God expects us to go forward doing the same. We are all "sons and daughters" of God.

Until this time in history, mankind has mainly followed by habitual patterns: what we are told, what we expect, what we think is supposed to be because it has happened to others, what religions have said, etc. But by changing the pattern, believing in the new paradigm, we open the door to new possibilities. For the last ten years, I have been willing to step out of the box to think for myself by using my intuitive insights, and I am now witnessing miracles. We are all co-creators with God. It is possible for us to become Beings of Light. We can then heal, and be healed. Praise be to God.

I prayed, "Thanks, God. I have finally been able to better understand what I know to be true and incorporate it with my faith. Hopefully, I am explaining it adequately enough for others to begin to understand. I now even better understand the reason Jesus gave us the Eucharist. The Eucharist is a constant reminder that He truly is with us all the time. If the intention of the priest and reciever are in unison, Christ is present for them. Thanks for the recent gift of seeing a Spirit bowing and kneeling by Fr. Thomas when he elevated the host at the consecration. Another affirmation!"

Heavenly Text

A friend gave me the book, *Quantum Theology, Spiritual Inplications of the New Physics,* written by a priest from England, Diarmuid O'Murchu. This gentleman is very articulate and knowledgeable, not only in religion but in physics. He uses scientific data to help explain what I have written. The book is a must read for anyone interested in where spirituality is going in the future.

April 2, 2007. While meditating and complaining that I had not had a vision for a long time, I suddenly had a vision of Mary. + I saw her from the bust up. She glowed with beauty, wore a veil, and was smiling at me. She then turned left and looked out a window. Then I saw, in the vision, a bird fly by. Mary then disappeared. End of vision. I exclaimed, "What was that about?"

I sat up in bed and turned to my left and to my surprise I saw a huge Barred owl sitting on a branch in the big old cedar tree outside our bedroom window. + Tears welled in my eyes and I recalled my long ago dream of the cedar tree.

Picking up my *Animal Speak* book once again I reread that an owl represents the mystery of magic, omens, silent wisdom, and visions in the night. I could relate. I feel like a messenger being led in the dark.

("Thanks for the message Mary. You know my life better than anyone. Once again I feel you nudging me along.")

I continued to see the owl daily for a few weeks which helped to remind me of my mission in life. Then, on April 22, when I looked out the window there were two Barred Owls sitting on the exact same cedar branch. My heart did a joyful jump remembering the messages from India and the two birds on a branch. I shed tears as I thanked God in heaven for another gift. I felt overwhelmed and watched the two owls sit

Heavenly Text

there for the entire day. I believe their appearance was telling me that I'm guided throughout the entire day and to never give up because - + *"I AM always with you"*.

When Erv came home, he also got to see the owls . As we looked out at them they began to hoot at us. Erv asked, "Have you ever been hooted at before?" What an experience! To me, it felt like a special blessing for us both.

I've written before: In mythology owls are omens and their presence presages a death of the old for the new to come to life. ("Thanks, God. I'm overwhelmed.)

April 13, 2007. I dreamed I was cleaning out the glove compartment and trunk of my car, in order to sell it. Then the scene changed to our family room and I saw a huge earthquake taking place. Everything was shaking. Erv walked over behind me and put his hands on my shoulders. End of dream.

Upon waking, as I thought about my dream I felt I was being informed that my car, my body, my transportation in life was being cleared and readied. I wondered for what?

For me, an earthquake is always a sign of big change. This time I was also being informed Erv is now totally embracing and standing behind me in what I do. He has slowly been coming around for years and I no longer feel his resistance to any of my friends or my work. Maybe the time has finally come. Did the owls help?

("Alleluia!! Thanks, God. Wonderful information, again on the 13th. Please lead the way. Where to go from here?")

May 21, 2007. We received a phone call about midnight telling us Mom had passed away in her sleep. Thanks be to God. She finally has gone home.

It was exactly nine months ago that she had what I called

Heavenly Text

her near death experience. Is her dying a new birthing-into eternal life? Something to think about.

("Thanks, God for finally taking her into your arms- home at last!")

Mom had recognized us immediately when we visited her in March. We got to actually visit for about ten minutes and then she bowed her head and appeared to sleep. We stayed awhile longer and when it was time to go I gave Mom a kiss and told her I loved her. I was shocked when she patted my arm and clearly said, "I know, Nancy, I know." + She said it with such a different voice that I felt it was a deep message- from her spirit-the last one I heard her utter. I believe she truly was letting me know she understood my destiny in life and understood. ("Thanks, God.")

June 15, 2007. A dream. I was with many individuals on the Labyrinth, when someone said, "There she is." Looking up everyone could see Mother Mary hovering above-a full moon brightly shining beside her. The feeling was awesome! + I recognized many of the individuals as they kept arriving to see the miracle.

Upon waking, I couldn't get over how the dream had felt very natural and real although this Labyrinth in the dream had a door to go though before you could walk it. I know a door in a dream symbolizes opportunity for growth. So, I presumed Mary was reaffirming the power of walking a Labyrinth and reminding me that "all have to walk through their own door in life to bring about their own personal growth." (Was this an affirmation about Mom's experiences? I think possibly so.)

I decided it was time to organize a group to walk the Labyrinth each month on the night of the full moon. (It rained that month on the night of the full moon but nine individuals

Heavenly Text
still showed up, and we walked it in the rain. Thanks, Mary.)

October 19, 2007. Today I witnessed the blossoming of a vessel for God to use and he is only thirteen years old. What a treat and gift to be present for this magnificent experience.

Eric's Mom had asked me a few weeks ago if she and Eric could come to learn how to do energy work. I had met Eric when he was undergoing chemotherapy treatments for cancer in his lymph glands several years before. At that time, his mother had asked if I would work on him. She brought him before his treatments began and for six months every time he had weekly or bi-weekly chemo. On our first visit, I casually suggested to Eric that he should bless the chemo before it was administered to him asking that the medicine do no harm to his body. Then I told him to try to watch the liquid as it went through his body asking that it be healing light to his lymph glands and not to harm or damage his organs. (I showed him pictures of the lymph system in the body.) I explained that after the treatment they could come to see me, and I would balance his body and try to energetically remove any chemo that his body did not need.

When he came after his first treatment I asked, "Did you see the medicine going into your body?" He replied, "Yep!" I congratulated him and told him to do that every time. Over the months we became friends of the heart as we worked together to try eliminate the cancer and restore health to his body. Eric did not lose his hair and seldom had very little nausea. In other words he did great. So far he has not had any re-occurrence of cancer and I feel confident he won't.

As I gave Eric his final hug after his last visit, I said, "Now Eric, don't forget me. Remember if you ever decide you want to do this work I think you would be good at it. Just call

Heavenly Text

me and I'll teach you." (I thought maybe in his twenties I would again hear from him.) I was more than thrilled when his Mom recently called. She had previously been so amazed with the energy work on Eric and had expressed then that she herself might like to learn.

Today, when they arrived I could hardly believe how the eleven year old kid was now a thirteen year old, tall young man. I first had his Mom lie on the table and showed Eric how to feel energy in her body. I then taught him how to administer hand placements to relax her body. I encouraged him to be still and listen to what the body was telling him. He did great.

About an hour later, it was his turn to lie on the table. I showed his Mom the same steps. When she layed her hand on his chest, he said, "Why am I seeing green?" I explained that he was probably seeing his heart chakra. I then placed my hand on his other chakras and he could tell me the correct color of all the chakras. (I recalled how my grandson had done that when he was five years old.) Then Eric surprised us by saying, "I now see my neck and there is a dark spot where I sprained it playing baseball a couple of weeks ago." His Mom and I placed our hands on his neck and he could see light coming from our hands desolving the spot. I then began asking him questions about other organs and was amazed how he could see whatever I asked him to. If he didn't know what it was, I would show him a picture from an anatomy book. He began giving clear discriptions of everything not only in his body but our bodies. (I was so delighted I wanted to jump out of my skin.) I kept glancing at his Mom who was utterly in awe. I told Eric that he was a wonderful seeing vessel and God was going to be able to use him to help many others. I told them that never in all the dozens of individuals I've taught has anyone be able to immediately "see". I kept telling him it was

Heavenly Text

a special gift. I warned him to never abuse the gift and he would become an amazing healer.

When we were finishing up our session, Erv came home and called for me to come to his aid. He informed me he thought he was passing another kidney stone, (Erv has had knidney stones in the past and anyone who has had one knows how terrible and uncomfortable passing one is.) I asked Eric if he could help me help Erv. Eric replied, "Sure, what does a kidney look like?" I showed him the picture of a kidney, the urethra tubes and the bladder. He immediately said, "I see there is something in the tube." I placed my hand where I thought the stone might be and Eric told me, "Put your hand down further. There, you are now on it. I can see the light from your hands moving it." As the stone moved Eric guided my hands and in hardly no time at all we had moved the stone into Erv's bladder. Amazed, and grateful Erv replied. "That's the first time that has ever gone that fast. He thanked us and went downstairs to try to empty the stone from his bladder- another painful process.

I assured Eric that his help had been exceptionally helpful, and his second sight was phenomenal. He replied, "I can still see another stone in Erv's kidney." (I thought to myself that Erv was not going to be happy to hear that.)

I explained to Eric that he had been unbelievable for his first day at learning energy work. (I wondered who would believe that he had helped someone pass a kidney stone.) I encourged him to keep up the good work and suggested we get together again soon to continue his progress.

Later that night Erv did pass another kidney stone. I had encourged him to drink lots of water for hours and the stone did pass rather quickly as I again guided it with my hands. To Erv it seemed a long time but having gone through this with

213

Heavenly Text

him before, I know this was by far the fastest yet.

("Thanks, God for an amazing afternoon. I remember Lisa saying: "You will pass this on to others." My heart was full of joy as I watched this young man open up to your power. I'm convinced all people have this gift and if they were encouraged and develope it when young, this would be a different world.")

October 23, 2007. The day of a spectacular spiritual experience.

Erv and I were privileged to be invited to attend the Interfaith Prayer Service with his holinesss the Dalai Lama at Indiana University. What an honor - only 400 invited guests for the service at St. Paul's Newman Center. We were fortunate enough to have reserved seats (to the left side of the altar). We were within 15 feet of the Dalai Lama for approximately an hour and a half. As I gazed at him, witnessed his huge smile and felt his presence, I thanked God over and over for this man's efforts in traveling the world with a message of peace. I kept mentally requesting that some of his energy and faith enter my being.

Beautiful music and singing began the service about 10:45am. I was immediately given a gift. As I heard bells ringing in the music, I suddenly started feeling pressure in my head like I feel when doing Spirit/energy work, but this was much stronger. I wondered what was about to transpire when I interiorly heard, *"The angels are arriving and filling this assembled space."* + I watched diligently, saw nothing, but in about three minutes, I heard *"Michael has arrived."* + (I presumed the message meant Archangel Michael.) Then a deep peace and quite entered my being. I was giving thanks, wondering if this meant the Dalai Lama was entering the

Heavenly Text

building. Soon, he was escorted in and the service began. ("Thanks angels for letting me feel your power and might.")

What a wonderful spiritual experience for all who attended this prayer service, one that we will hold dear in our hearts. I'm still floating high as I write this on the 25th.

November 2007. I read the book *The Mayan Code*. I was intrigued how the author, Barbara Clow, through personal extensive study and numerous writings discovered the calendar's many encoded messages. She describes how high energy is flooding the earth at this time and gives her interpretation of the alignment of the earth with the center of the Milky Way. Clow explains how the Mayan calendar is a record of our recorded evolution and transformation of consciousness, ending in 2012. I was thrilled to discover that recent turning points in our evolution, according to the Mayan Calendar were the same dates as many of my visions over the years - amazing affirmation of my education from the heavens. I excitely await further information.

February 20. 2008. Erv got the flu which progressed into pneumonia. He had a terrible cough. One day while coughing he passsed out. I rushed to his side while praying to Spirit. When he came to he said, "What are you doing?" When I explained he had passed out, his comment was, "I was only dreaming." Later the doctor called Erv's coughing "tuss syncope" or faint coughing. I'd never heard of that before.

Erv passed out a total of eight times over several days. It was a scary site to see his eyes roll back and him to be out for a few minutes each time. Each time, upon awakening, he would say, "I was only dreaming." He did tell me a couple of times that he thought he was dying in the dream. I don't know what

Heavenly Text

this was all about, but seemed to me God was preparing him for something.

March 20, 2008. Erv was cleaning out the gutter on the front porch, and when coming down the ladder he missed the last step, lost his balance and fell backwards. He hit his head on the corner of the house and was knocked out. I "happened to be" walking past the front window and saw it happen. I rushed out as I called on the angels for help. He was totally out for about five minutes during which time I rushed into the house, grabbed the phone and called a neighbor.

Erv was coming to about the time the neighbor arrived and knew absolutely nothing. He didn't remember falling, who the neighbor was, etc. He had no recall of the immediate past or any questions I asked him about the last few weeks. I called the doctor and he said to go to the emergency room and request a cat scan and EKG.

Meanwhile, I called my seer friends to find out that Erv was "bleeding in the brain." Later, the cat scan proved them right. After the emergency room they put Erv in ICU and began more tests. (I worked on Erv, seeing light surroundiing his head the entire time.) Later that day when they did an angiogram of the brain the bleeding had stopped. Before they got Erv back from the test to ICU, my friend had called and told me the bleeding had stopped.

Upon returning to ICU from his angiogram Erv said to the nurse on call, "I told the docs doing the tests I was sure I was OK because my wife is a healer and she probably had taken care of it by now." (I was shocked and beamed. Thanks, God. What a difference in his attitude from years ago. I doubt he remembers saying those words, but the angels sure used him to get the message to many. I wondered if all his recent medical

Heavenly Text

experiences been the releasing of past lives? Thanks, God. Thanks for the healing! Having medical intuitive friends is such a gift. I wish doctors would use medical intuitives rather than all of the invasive testing.)

Erv came home in two days but had to return a week later for another round of tests to satisfy the doctors. If it would have been me, I would have passed on the later tests; but Erv is not as confident in my friends' abilities as I am - yet. I knew he was fine and just kept thanking heaven

March 27, 2008. The first visit of a young man about thirty years old proved very interesting. While I was working on him he said, "Nancy, this is very strange, I have my eyes closed but I can still see you." I instructed him to ask to see inside my head-to see my brain. Surprised he said, "I see it!" I then suggested he look at my heart. "Ican see it," he joyfully exclaimed!" Then I told him to look at his own heart and several other organs. I then suggested he look at my spiritual body. He shouted with joy, "I see your aura, your chakras, there real!" I was elated for him. Another person awakening to the gift of seeing. Mankind is opening up more and more and it appears rapidly on my table.

(Thanks, God. I know more and more are awakening to your Spirit. Thanks, for letting me be a part of this process. I feel so full of joy!") The young man returned in another week and I helped him learn to ask questions to better establish a rapport with Spirit.

April 18 thru 21, 2008. A fabulous experience. Along with three girl friends I went to Chicago for a Matrix Energetics workshop with Richard Bartlett, D.C., N.D. I have mentioned Dr. Bartlett briefly in past writings. He is also very

Heavenly Text

knowledgeable in physics. What an experience. He taught over 200 individuals in attendance how to retrieve frequency in the morphic field and give to others for physical and emotional healings. I believe he has found more answers to how Jesus preformed His healings-something we can all do-just as Jesus said, "You can do what I do and even more."

Richard is a very joyful, full of life, happy, brilliant, man who shares his stories and teaches others how to join in on use the resonance in the morphic field that surrounds us all. He says that what ever has happened or has been learned by anyone can be borrowed and used by all of us. All present were able to join in the fun. He was so child-like and funny that we laughed for three days. He often said, "If you can dream it, you can do it." He stressed that, "We were learning to create and transform reality at the quantum level." I think it will take practice to incorporate what I learned from him with what I already do; but I know his teachings will enhance my healing work.

July 10th through the 13th we were in St. Louis at our daughter's house. Deanna asked me to work on Madison (7years old) becasue she had an unexplainable rash. What an experience! While my hands were on her she began exclaiming, "Danny, I'm seeing so many colors. She enthusiastically described seeing colors in all shapes and sizes. "Awesome!" she exclaimed! "Now, I see purple rain. Now I see lightning. Now I see an orange straight line. Now I see popcorn," and on and on she went. My heart was bursting with joy. She was so excited and happy that it was contageous. Afterwards she could see all of our auras. I thanked God over and over for her awakening to the energy in her body and in her visions. (And thankfully her rash diasappeared.)

Heavenly Text

I then showed Madison Matrix Energetics and she began to do it. She was terrific at it. What joy! I know it is time for all to become awakened to God's future plan for us, and I was fortunate enough to experience it with my granddaughter. We are on the cutting edge of wonderful happenings from the heavens!

July 14, 2008. When I went to make coffee, I was surprised to spot another hawk sitting outside on my deck. It remained for sometime. I tried to communicate with it. The next morning two hawks were sitting side by side on my deck. Now what are the chances of that? I was elated. I recalled my message of the birds sitting side by side that I received from the Bhakti message and the many times I've experienced seeing two birds on the same branch. I cannot explain the peace and calm I felt throughout my body as I watched them remain sitting in the sun for me to admire. I whispered, "Thanks God for the gift. I know you have not forsaken me and are always with me."

Each morning for a week the two hawks came to visit. What a joyous blessing.

When Madison came for her summer visit the next week she was thrilled to see a hawk up close. I wondered. Were these visits from the hawks just letting me know she was going to follow in my footsteps?

October 13, 2008. Another wonderful gift on the 13th. A spiritual blessing from the heavens. Another Domincan priests, Father Simon, who now presides at the Newman Center (replacing Father Joachim) came to experience Spirit/energy work. I tried to quickly tell him about my fifteen years of seeing visions and working for God with my healing ministry.

Heavenly Text

We had a wonderful session. After balancing his energy Simon's arm began to release long held pain. He informed me that he had experienced pain in his left shoulder and arm for months. As our time together passed Father Simon spoke up and said, "I think I am supposed to tell you I feel the energy of St. Francis here in this room beside you." I asked him to explain how he knew, "I often feel the presence and energy of individuals and just know who it is." I replied, "I have a relic of St. Francis here in this room." He then siad, "I also feel the presence of St. Dominic."

My heart leaped with joy because as far as I could tell Fr. Simon must be Claircognizant. (Claircognizant is when information comes to someone with flashes of knowing.)

My heart was so full of joy it was about to explode. I believe this information is what I have been waiting to hear. Definitely, I am to work with "all" the Dominican priests.

("Thank you, God, Thank you! Thank you, Mary. At last, a priest who will understand what is happening to me. I can hardly believe you have finally sent me the Dominicans to convey your information. No wonder all the messages about Sts. Francis and Dominic over the years. Now, please remain by my side as I try to convey to them what I know to be true.")

December 2008. Erv came home from his yearly check up from his heart doctor with the news that the doctor wanted him to get an ultra sound on his carotid artery. The doctor said it sounded clogged. I immediately called three of my seer friends and each said,"Yes, it is very clogged. He will probably be having surgery next week."

I took Erv upstairs to work on him. While working on him he said, "Do you see angels? I feel them here." I did not see them but felt something profound was happening.

Heavenly Text

That Wednesday when he went in for the ultra sound the technician said, "I don't know why the doctor had you to come in, your arteries are clear."
(Thanks, God. I'm astounded every time. But this was extra special. Erv has finally joined me in thought. Together we will go forward. Thank you, thank you.)

January 2009. Working jigsaw puzzles has long been a hobby of mine--the harder the better, but even I was questioning my abilities when I received a Christmas gift from Erv, a 2000 piece puzzle depicting the "Last Supper" painted by Leonardo DaVinci. I had fallen and cracked a bone in my left heel earlier in the fall which was not healing properly. I needed to totally stay off of it and Erv said, "This will give you something to do."

I didn't even have a table big enough to hold the 38" x 26" puzzle and all of its pieces. So Erv cut a big piece of plywood to put over our game table and I began. Initially it was a chore just sorting the 2000 different dark pieces into bowls. All the border pieces were navy blue so it was imposssible to put the border together first. The puzzle was going to have to be worked from inside out. I told the Dominican priests that I would give it to them to hang in their chapel in their new rectory, if and when it was completed. When I began it the first week in January, I announced, "If I don't have this done by Easter, it comes down."

It took a lot of patience and time, more work than fun. Some days I worked at it for six hours. I surprised myself and completed it in three weeks. Upon completing the puzzle, I was terribly disappointed because a piece was missing. Erv and I searched everywhere, even moving furniture, without any luck finding it. We have no animals and no one else is around. I

Heavenly Text

could not imagine how this had happened. I begged my angels to find it!

I told the Dominicans and it was decided that I should seal the puzzle with a glaze and just put a brass plaque over the empty space, which happened to be at the top in the center. Erv began making the frame.

Several days passed and one night I had a vision about the puzzle. In the vision I saw myself place the missing puzzle piece into the puzzle. Then I saw a cat run across the table. Upon awakening I told Erv I thought Pam was going to bring back the missing piece. (You may recall the story of Tiger that I wrote about in *Heavenly Text, Vol. I.* How three years after Pam died she brought back our lost cat. So seeing the cat made me think Pam must be involved.)

The next day I was terribly disappointed when the piece did not show up.

In the middle of February I decided to work on another puzzle. Erv was with me when I cut a sealed new box and dumped the pieces on the table. As we sorted the pieces for the border, I noticed a dark piece that did not seem to match the colors of this puzzle, which was fish in water. As I worked the puzzle I kept wondering where that piece was going to go. Then when the puzzle was about completed it suddenly came to my awareness, "Could this piece be the missing piece from my other puzzle? Surely not!" I ran to the basement to the other puzzle and sure enough, it was the missing piece. + I screamed with wonder and delight. I thought impossible, but it fit perfectly. Two different puzzles, from two different companies and this last box was sealed. I excitedly ran to tell Erv and he said, "That has to be a miracle. I looked everywhere for that piece." I smiled and said, "Pam did it again."

I wondered what the Dominicans would think of a gift of a

Heavenly Text

"miracle puzzle."

Fifteen minutes later, Fr. Thomas just happened to stop by. Coincidene? I think not. Erv immediately announced, "We just had a miracle." Father was stunned and announced, "You know the original picture of *"The Last Supper"* by DaVinci hangs in a Dominican convent in Spain. +

I wrote this story and glued it to the back of the puzzle so future generations would know the story of the miracle. There was also a piece missing in the completed fish puzzle. How appropriate to help complete "The Last Supper."

("Thank you, thank you to the heavens for this wonderful adventure and miracle. How you traded the pieces I'll never know, but I am elated. This once again confirms what I know to be true. Dead people can communicate with us. It has happened to me many times.")

Going to the Light

There has been another gap in my writings – eighteen months to be exact. Much has been going on, so it is time to get it all on paper. It is now July 2010. I remember writing earlier that the years from 2000 to 2010 were going to be major years of change, and it certainly has been for me. I have once again been more enlightened by Spirit. I know wisdom lessons will never end and I thank God daily that Erv has finally come around to a deeper respect for Spirit/energy work. He also has a greater respect for construction work, because since 1993 he has helped build over 100 houses for Habitat for Humanity.

You have previously read how I see and communicate with Spirit. How my journey with spirit began at an apparition site when I saw Mother Mary. Once I acknowledged the Spirit world, it began to communicate with me: visions, prophetic dreams, visitations with Pam, and later communications with Jesus.

You have read how over the years I have "seen" bodies of light, "spirits." Usually, at funerals I still see the spirits of individuals who have died, attending their own funerals. I feel the presence of loved ones around individuals when I work on them. At times, I release spirits that seem to be stuck and cannot find their way to the Light. I sometimes feel spirits go through me. All of this has been going on spontaneously for years. Recently this has become more pronounced.

I believe most people are confused how reality and non-reality work together. Religions and society speak of a heaven and a hell. I think this is what has created much misunderstanding in our world and the spirit world. I think

Heavenly Text

most people believe when they die, they will simply go to one or the other. I personally do not believe there is a hell, because I do not believe God, who is all love, would ever punish anyone. I think we create our own hell by the way "we learn" or "do **not** learn." I now know there are many "lost souls" in the spirit world or on "another dimension" because of this misunderstanding. I now believe when one dies, it is necessary to pray and ask to "go to the Light." I have learned that we get to come here on earth, over and over, to learn our lessons. We have lost sight of the reasons we were created, and what life is about. Life is supposed to be about growing and becoming more spiritual. Life is about finding Christ within - then "going to the Light," our home.

Over the years, I have not given much thought to negative energy but this past year, Spirit wanted me to learn more about this and is asking me to write what I now know to be true.

I wrote earlier how last year I cracked a bone in my foot, the calcaneus of my left heel. I fell while walking on the trail. It was more serious than I originally thought and it took over a year to heal. After my heel finally healed, I had another major problem, a major back problem. At first, I thought my back hurt because I had walked unevenly with the heel problem. Not so. The pain in my back kept getting worse and worse. Excruciating is the best way to describe the pain. Energy work from my co-workers did not seem to help. Going to the doctor did not help either. I had individuals praying for and with me, priests laid hands on me, but nothing seemed to budge the problem. After a chiropractor visit, doctor visits, many x-rays, and an MRI, no one could figure out the problem. I became quite frustrated. Then I saw a therapist. She took one look at my back and said, "You have a torqued spine." She explained, "When muscles get extremely tight in the back it torques the spine. X-ray type of equipment does not pick up on muscle problems." She administered "strain, counter strain" and I was 90% better. This process was amazing. I still had pain but I

Heavenly Text

could handle it. It had been a month of trauma. I was perplexed and kept wondering "why?"

Then God stepped in-in a big way, and I realized what my learning lesson was. Again, Spirit was teaching me. This time about negative spirit attachments. My wisdom lessons have always been from experience. This was no exception. I'll explain:

I received a call from a minister of a Christian church (Disciples of Christ) from another town who wanted to know if he could bring someone to meet me. The minister had heard from another mutual minister friend that I received visions. This minister had a church member who was experiencing visions who was anxious to talk to someone who would understand. I remember how confused I felt when my visions started so I was happy to see them. The minister, his wife, the gentleman in question, and his wife, all came together. We discussed visions for several hours. Then I asked if they would like to see where I have my healing ministry. On the way to my room the minister remarked, "Recently I've discovered I have the gift of healing. Several times when visiting patients in the hospital when I've prayed over them my hands have become incredibly hot and afterwards the individuals have gotten better." "That's wonderful," I exclaimed. " So you will easily understand what I do. I call the work I do Spirit/energy work because I know God does the work - **I am just a vessel**. I have learned how we are all energy and light and I have learned how to manipulate energy."

When they began to depart, I suddenly found myself saying, "Since you have the gift of healing would you lay hands on my back? I've been fighting back pain for over a month." He had me lie on my massage table, on my stomach, and he began to pray over me. I could feel my back vibrating and reacting to his words and prayers. I began to laugh and said out loud, "This is a riot. You all came to learn from me and here I'm the one on the table." He asked if I had any holy

Heavenly Text

oil. I pointed to where the oil was. I heard him pray, "Come out. Come out." (Obviously, he felt the problem was a possession. I was wondering, "how that could have happened?")

My back vibrated some more and, bingo, all went still and quiet. I was thrilled when I got off the table that there was **no** more pain. We thanked God and they were on their way. Immediately after they left, I began searching scripture to find where Jesus had commanded, "Come out!" I wondered if all of my back pain had actually originated from a negative source. I had recently been reading more about releasing spirits and wondered if God had let this happen to me so I would learn even more. I was very perplexed how and why all of this had come about. The pattern of my learning has always been, experience something, read about it, put it into practice. I recalled back in 1996 when Jesus told me:

+"*Nancy, you are doing fine. You learned what I wanted you to today. Do not be afraid. Know I'm with you. I'm working with more and more people. You will be needed in many capacities. Continue to learn.*

You are a thought form, My thought. If one's thoughts are in unison with Me when they die I can use them again. If not, they go elsewhere or remain amongst you. Then those thoughts need an entrance into heaven. The work Lavern does helps those thoughts to find Me again in order to continue on as a new thought for Me. My plan is vast. My numbers/thoughts are many. It is not your job to understand it all. Just know that each individual is My thought, My soul extension, My work, being utilized in order to bring the unity and oneness that I see for creation.

Now that you work with My Light, your Spirit self reaches out, collects, and engulfs thoughts for Me daily. When the majority of individuals reach the fullness of Light and life, all will be full of Light. There will be no greed, rebuff or despair.

Heavenly Text
All negative-ness, all darkness, will be gone. All will be at peace in My Light, and creation will flourish like never before.

Nancy, put on your armor of Light daily and continue to be one with Me. Read your Bible now. Look up the readings on healing and expelling demons."

***

I now know that Jesus knew I needed to refresh my memory and to experience what I had been taught years ago in order to fully comprehend. The next day my pain was still gone. I had fun when I went to church reminding my priest friends that their prayers had not worked but the minister's had. "I've always known it makes no different what religion one belongs to. God can work with any and all," I gleefully exclaimed.

The next day, I called a spiritualist, who resides in Canada. I had recently read that she specializes in releasing spirits. I told her I wanted to learn more and she suggested I read three books.

1. *Remote Depossession* is written by a deceased Osteopath, Irene Hickman, D.O. Irene learned how to communicate with spirit thru hypnosis. She learned to release negative spirits with Michael the Archangel, and clearly describes how to do this. After reading about releasing lost souls and helping them "go to the Light," the process became easier for me. (Anyone interested in this process can order Irene's book at docirene@hickman-healing-foundation.org)

2. *Thirty Years with the Dead* by Carl Wickland, M.D., is a book written 150 years ago by a physiatrist who worked in a mental hospital. His wife was a medical intuitive and could "see" and "communicate" with spirits. When he administered shock treatments to the mentally ill, his wife would see spirits come out. She would talk to these spirits and help them "go to the Light." This book has many stories about this process.

Heavenly Text
3. *Your Immortal Body of Light* by Mitchell Earl Gibson, M.D. is a book about a doctor who does deep meditation. He meditates and lifts himself out of his body. He then roams the hospital halls and helps "lost souls" go to the Light.

I heard of another healer, Vianna Stibal, and purchased her books on *Theta Healing*. Vianna cured herself of bone cancer. She has also been taught and guided by the Spirit world. I believe we are both vessels that God uses but she explained healing possibilities that I did not know existed. Years ago Jeanne had previously taught me SER but Vianna's way is much easier and quicker. I know being a vessel for healings all comes down to intention - "**ask and you shall receive**." But it had never dawned on me to clear one's subconscious of generations of past memories or one's DNA by simply **asking**. Vianna explains in detail how to do this. I've incorporated her information into my Spirit/energy work.

(Thanks, God, for the confirmation of my past experiences of clearing generational memories through experiences. Although it took me years I now know and can quickly help others. Thank you, thank you.)

I also read *Deliverance from Evil Spirits* by Francis MacNutt, which is written by an ex-Dominican priest. Interesting!

Wow! What wonderful information all these books contained. I already knew that when we die we step out of our bodies but I did not realize how "many" individuals simply get "lost" and don't know what to do or where to go. Often when reading these books I recalled Pam's last words. "I see Christ Light." (When one knows Christ within, the Light is readily available.) I now know God definitely wanted me to learn more about "lost souls."

I immediately asked my "seers" to see if they could see

Heavenly Text

"lost souls" and to all of our amazement they could. I wondered why we had not thought to ask to see "lost souls" before? Again, "**Ask and it will be given unto you,**" was readily available to us. We just did not know to ask.

The "seers" could immediately distinguish between positive (souls of light) and negative souls (souls of darkness). I asked how they looked and how could they tell the difference from "lost souls" and those that had already gone to the Light.

One "seer" said, "I know they are negative when they appear dark, angry and confused. Those that have crossed over look bright, clear, happy."

Another "seer" said, "When they have crossed over, they feel and look complete. They're brilliant, glowing, and have a white essence. The "lost souls" look fuzzy, bewildered and confused. They just look like they are on a different dimension. The dark negative ones have no white light and usually are angry."

Another "seer" said, "Sometimes I see them only in or around the aura, like a cloud, and sometimes I see them inside the body of a person. I feel them and know if they are good or bad." I could totally relate to that statement.

Another medical intuitive and "seer" told me that she thinks souls stay and hang around, because they think they can continue to work through others to finish what they did not get finished while in their body. She said, "I try to explain to them that they will be more effective if they go to the Light first, and then come back to help. I also think that those who cannot cross over are strong willed individuals who do not operate from their heart, but from their head. Usually these are individuals who still have their personality they had on earth. Legal and money matters are very strong in them. If one believes in going to the Light they have no problems. One just has to ask, "to go to the *Light.*" Some do not even know they are dead."

Heavenly Text

It is very evident that many individuals do not know they are dead. We soon discovered some souls return to their families, which at times may cause problems or an illness in a family member. Sometimes a family member cannot "let a deceased member go" and this causes a soul to remain on this earthly dimension. A "lost soul" unintentionally drains the energy of an individual when they attach to one's aura. This is definitely not the reason for all illness but it does account for some. At times negative souls gather in groups and attach to individuals-this is often when mental problems develop. We were learning how this interaction with the Spirit world was greater and more prevalent than we thought.

When souls know God and **ask** to "go to the Light" they easily cross over. Then they learn lessons on the other side and eventually reincarnate in order to further help themselves and others. Negative, dark souls roam the spirit world not knowing **how** to "go to the Light" or do **not want** to "go to the Light," and can cause great havoc. This is what many may call the devil. I call all these patterns **positive** and **negative** energy, "lost souls" learning from each other. Jesus called them "thought forms." It is the cycle of life. It has now been proven to me--time and time again.

I think Christianity does not understand this problem. It is a very simple process to release spirits once you know they are present. One simply calls on Michael the Archangel who helps the person "go to Light" or go to a place where they can learn to "go to the Light." (Could this "lost time" be what some call purgatory?) It is very simple to help the "lost souls," **positive** or **negative** ones. My "seers" have seen Archangel Michael releasing souls over and over again.

I want to explain how we first discovered how effective this process works. Dottie was here and I told her I wanted to try to release some suspected negative energy from someone at a distance. This person was bi-polar and I suspected negative

Heavenly Text

energy. I told her I had read how to do this. She had not read the book written by Irene Hickman. Dottie got relaxed on the massage table and I gave her the name of the person. She saw the person, asked the person's permission to help him, and we began. I said, "Call in Michael the Archangel." She replied, "He's here. And he has a net." I laughed and said, "You are ahead of me." The next step is you are suppose to ask him to bring his net." I then instructed her to ask Michael to put the negative spirit in his net. She replied, "That was quick. It is in the net." I then instructed her to ask Michael to take the person to a place to learn to "go to the Light." She saw the person leave. We were thrilled. We thanked God over and over. We asked if there were other lost spirits around for them to also leave. (That day there was only one. But since then she sometime sees several dark patterns leave.) We were surprised and amazed how easy and simple it was, and we knew it would be something we would be doing often.

Now when I sense a presence while doing Spirit/energy work I call on Archangel Michael and go through the process. We are discovering that "sometimes" when people are having a hard time healing this is definitely the problem–they have an attachment. Prior to this I have at times felt souls passing through me, but now I know I need to be more observant of their presence. I still wondered **how** and **why** one "lost soul" had decided to attach to me.

Then within days, I met Mike, a gentleman who had cured himself from a disability by using EFT (Emotional Freedom Technique). There is lots of info about this healing technique on the web. Mike was helpful in explaining to me that if one does not "**daily**" ground oneself properly and then surround them selves with an "**armor of Light,**" one opens oneself up to attachments. I know I had not been doing this to myself when doing Spirit/energy as **much** and as **often** as I should. I

Heavenly Text

had learned this long ago but had become careless. I'll add the process I use here.

***

I stand with my feet planted firmly on the floor. With my eyes closed I pray ask "with intention," for the earth to share its energy with me. I relax my feet and I begin to feel the earth's energy come up my legs, go through the trunk of my body, go up though my neck and out the top of my head. I ask the energy to go all the way up to God in the heavens.

Then "with intention," I pray and ask God to fill me with His love and Light. I feel His Spirit energy come down into the top of my head, go down the truck of my body, and go down my legs into the ground. I then ask the energy of the earth and the energy of the heavens to swirl within, cleansing and strengthening me. Sometimes the energy becomes so strong my body becomes a vortex and I can hardly remain standing.

Then "with intention," I spin my root chakra clockwise and ask it to go down deep into the earth (like a drill), visualizing this happening as it goes down through the inside of my leg, through the ground, bedrock, water, soil, etc. When well grounded, my feet feel heavy. I then bring the energy back up to my heart and crown and ask to be balanced.

Then "with intention," I reach to the sun and ask for a beam of Light. I imagine this beam miles above me, going through my body and chakras, down into the earth, miles below me. I ask my angels and guides to spin this beam of Light clockwise out around me to form an armor of Light to protect me from all negative energies and individuals from any source.

I pray and ask that my Light shine through this protective armor of Light to all that I encounter. Then I say the prayer Jesus taught me in 1995. + *"Our Father, who art in heaven, be*

Heavenly Text

with me daily. Guide me. Lead me. Surround my heart with Your angels. Speak to me softly and gently. Help me to hear Your whispers. My love goes out to others because of Your love for me. When alone or in a crowd calm my heart to hear Your words. Be forever with me, by my side, to guide me in Your ways. Help me to be a beacon for others, to radiate Your love, to make You known to all mankind."

***

Now I knowingly release Spirits regularly. I help them go to the Light. It is such a supreme gift to help others this way. We generally work in pairs as it makes the energy stronger. What I do know, if one does not "see" but "feels" spirits present it still works. I strongly encourage others to know, that they are legitimate even if they don't "see," because I don't and it works for me. The "seers, have confirmed my work. I recall --"You believe because you see me. Happy are those who have not seen and yet believe." (John 20:29)

Examples of recent releases:

One day a friend called and said her son, Ted, (9) was acting so strange, angry, not able to sleep-just not himself. They had recently moved and she wondered if he just missed his old surroundings. She had taken him to the doctor who wanted to give him medicine and she called me first. I had one of my "seers" look in and sure enough he had an attached negative spirit. We thought possibly from the new house. We cleared the negative energy around him and made sure no more were in the house. He improved and was his old self immediately. Two weeks later my friend called and said Ted was acting strange again. Sure enough we found another attachment. I said, "We must have missed something." We cleared him and the house again. Then I had an intuitive thought to check his classroom at school. My "seer" saw many

Heavenly Text
around his school. As we cleared them from the school dozens began to come out of the ground. We decided the school must have been built on an old gravesite, battleground, or Indian burial site. What an experience! I bet the teacher is much happier!

A lady came to see me who had been ill for many years. The doctors had diagnosised her as having fibromyolgia, but she was not responding to the medicine and was in constant pain. I asked her when the problem had started. She replied, "About ten years ago when my dad died." Immediately, I suspected an attachment, either she was still holding on to him or he was attaching and was lost. I called on Archangel Michael and within minutes she asked, "What are you doing? It feels like you are lifting something off of me." I tried my best to explain without upsetting her. She left pain free.

I pray, "Thanks, God; you never cease to amaze me with my education. I did not enjoy the pain of an attachment but I certainly learned that negative energy or "lost souls/energy" is here among us, more than I thought. I now realize as the earth is renewing itself, we can help renew the spirit world by teaching "lost souls" how to "go to the Light." I believe this lesson was an important lesson that I needed to re-learn and to pass o to others..

I know we are all trying to come into balance here on earth and in the spirit world, so that we can all evolve into a higher consciousness. I now better understand how your creation is a cycle repeating itself, as we evolve into what you want us to be. Thanks for guiding the way. How did this attachment happen to me? From where or from whom? I'm not sure. But I am definitely being more attentive protecting myself from taking on any negative energy, from others here on earth, or from the spirit world. I had become careless in grounding and surrounding myself with Your Light. Please

Heavenly Text
help me to continue to work for you and with you. I love you-as you love me. Thank you, over and over, for being my guiding Light."

***

As I journey my path and have written about my personal life, I have often felt alone. Spirit gradually sent me individuals along the way to educate and encourage me. What was confusing has become more clear. Whether it is religion, science, or medicine, it seems to me that we're all looking for the same thing, a balance in our lives, a balance with nature, a balance with the Divine. I believe this is what Christ did. I believe Christ was Divine and showed us how we can become Divine.

The truth is, we are all children of God. The truth is, Christ expects us to love ourselves and to love one another. The truth is, He wants the hearts of men in union with the heart of God. The truth is, we are all one. The truth is, we all can find Him within.

When mankind realizes the truth, and each takes part in the personal education of his/her own soul, the world will become a different place. I can testify that the Spirit world is patiently waiting in the wings to help each and every one if they but ask. My advice to all, "Let Spirit feed you." If it happened for me, it can happen for anyone."

"If you do not believe, you will not understand." Isaiah 7:9

About the Author

I write for God. He is the "Presence" in my life. I began to write at the request of my daughter who, when she was dying of leukemia, insisted I was to write a book. I agreed I would try some day, but little did I know it was going to be an on-going event. I started out slowly and there has been a building of experiences. In time I started receiving hundreds of unsolicited visions and messages from heaven that guide my writings. I have kept everything in chronological order that has been relayed to me over many years (1985-2010) – thus three volumes.

Humankind is evolving into a higher consciousness. We have forgotten as a whole that we are all "one" and are here on earth to evolve spiritually. We are living in unprecedented times when all of creation is trying to come into balance - a balance in our bodies, a balance with the earth, and a balance with the heavens.

I had to learn that the chaos of this world and my life were but a gift to enable me to grow. It hasn't always been easy, but it has been a wonderful journey. I learned to pay attention to the synchronicity occurrences and intuitive insights in my life. I now receive messages in prayer, meditation, prophetic dreams, visions and experiences throughout the day when encountering a profoundness that demands to be recognized. In time I learned to become an open vessel for the power of God to manifest through me. Laying-on-of-hands and other healing modalities became a part of my life. Knowing and believing in God's power is the key to eternal life.